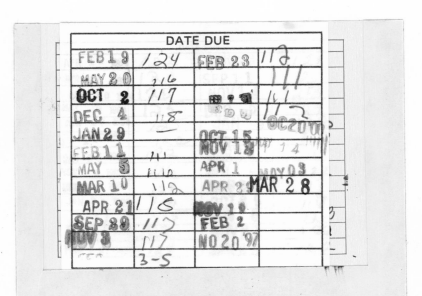

DATE DUE			
FEB 19	124	FEB 23	112
MAY 20	216		111
OCT 2	117		141
DEC 4	118		162
JAN 29	—	OCT 15	
FEB 11	111	NOV 18	14
MAY 5	1110	APR 1	MAY 03
MAR 10	112	APR 29	MAR 28
APR 21	118	NOV 18	
SEP 30	117	FEB 2	
NOV 3	117	NO 20 97	
FEB	3-5		

996.9   Carpenter, Allan.
C

          Hawaii.

The New
Enchantment of America
HAWAII

By Allan Carpenter

CHILDRENS PRESS, CHICAGO

ACKNOWLEDGMENTS

For assistance in the preparation of the revised edition, the author thanks:
JOHN G. SIMPSON, President, Hawaii Visitors Bureau, and LINDY BOYES, Senior Communications Specialist, Hawaii Visitors Bureau.

American Airlines—Anne Vitaliano, Director of Public Relations; *Capitol Historical Society*, Washington, D. C.; *Newberry Library,* Chicago, Dr. Lawrence Towner, Director; *Northwestern University Library*, Evanston, Illinois; *United Airlines*—John P. Grember, Manager of Special Promotions; Joseph P. Hopkins, Manager, News Bureau; Carl Provorse, *Carpenter Publishing House.*

UNITED STATES GOVERNMENT AGENCIES: *Department of Agriculture*—Robert Hailstock, Jr., Photography Division, Office of Communication; Donald C. Schuhart, Information Division, Soil Conservation Service. *Army*—Doran Topolosky, Public Affairs Office, Chief of Engineers, Corps of Engineers. *Department of Interior*—Louis Churchville, Director of Communications; EROS Space Program—Phillis Wiepking, Community Affairs; Charles Withington, Geologist; Mrs. Ruth Herbert, Information Specialist; Bureau of Reclamation; National Park Service—Fred Bell and the individual sites; Fish and Wildlife Service—Bob Hines, Public Affairs Office. *Library of Congress*—Dr. Alan Fern, Director of the Department of Research; Sara Wallace, Director of Publications; Dr. Walter W. Ristow, Chief, Geography and Map Division; Herbert Sandborn, Exhibits Officer. *National Archives*—Dr. James B. Rhoads, Archivist of the United States; Albert Meisel, Assistant Archivist for Educational Programs; David Eggenberger, Publications Director; Bill Leary, Still Picture Reference; James Moore, Audio-Visual Archives. *United States Postal Service*—Herb Harris, Stamps Division.

For assistance in the preparation of the first edition, the author thanks:
Dr. Donald Mitchell, Head, Hawaiian Department, the Kamehameha Schools; James R. McDonough, Executive Secretary, Hawaiian Education; Department of Planning and Economic Development; Pineapple Growers Association of Hawaii; Hawaiian Sugar Growers Association; Chamber of Commerce of Honolulu; Hawaiian Historical Society.

Illustrations on the preceding pages:
Cover photograph: Hanuma Bay, Oahu, Hawaii Visitors Bureau
Page 1: Commemorative stamps of historic interest
Pages 2-3: Grass shack on Oahu, Hawaii, American Airlines
Page 3: (Map) USDI Geological Survey
Pages 4-5: Honolulu area, EROS Space Photo, USDI Geological Survey, EROS Data Center

Project Editor, Revised Edition:
Joan Downing
Assistant Editor, Revised Edition:
Mary Reidy

6 7 8 9 10 11 12 R 85 84 83

Library of Congress Cataloging in Publication Data
Carpenter, John Allan, 1917-
Hawaii.

(His The new enchantment of America)
SUMMARY: An introduction to the Aloha State, including its history, resources, famous citizens, and places of interest.
1. Hawaii—Juvenile literature.
[1. Hawaii] I. Title. II. Series.
DU623.2.C37   996.9'03   79-9991
ISBN 0-516-04111-8

Contents

A True Story to Set the Scene

THE BATTLE OF NIIHAU

At about 2:00 P.M. on December 7, 1941, a Japanese plane crash-landed on the Hawaiian island of Niihau, and its pilot became the first Japanese invader of American soil in World War II. The events that followed illustrate once again the extraordinary variety of things that combine to create the enchantment of Hawaii.

At the time of the crash, much of the United States Pacific Fleet lay in ruins at Pearl Harbor, and most of the world knew about the attack. Not the island of Niihau, however, even though it lies only about 140 miles (225 kilometers) from Honolulu. There were no telephones or radios on the island to give its two hundred native residents news. Up to this time the island had remained much as it had been for hundreds of years, almost untouched by modern civilization.

Into this quiet paradise suddenly crashed modern civilization at its worst—war! The islanders knew that something had to be wrong, and a cowboy, Hawila Kaleohano, disarmed the pilot and took his papers. One of the island's owners, Aylmer Robinson, was at the family home on Kauai, so the people decided to keep the pilot prisoner until they could reach Robinson.

However, the pilot escaped with the help of a Japanese beekeeper named Harada, who lived on the island. He recaptured his arms and, using the plane's machine guns, began to spray the village with bullets. Most of the people fled to caves. The pilot was determined to retrieve and destroy his papers. Apparently they contained military secrets. The pilot and Harada went to Kaleohano's house but he saw them coming and got away. They invaded the home of elderly Mrs. Huluoulani and threatened to kill her if she did not tell them where

Opposite: The island of Niihau, where the "Battle of Niihau" was fought on December 7, 1941, is in the background. The Japanese pilot probably had a similar view of the "Mysterious Island" before he crashed. The tiny uninhabited island of Lehua shows clearly in the foreground.

to find Kaleohano or the papers. Calmly reading her Bible, Mrs. Huluoulani refused to answer. The two men left and then ransacked the village, setting fire to Kaleohano's house, but they could not find the papers.

Meanwhile, a group of the islanders was rowing to Kauai for help, but a local leader, Benihakaka Kanahele, and his wife suddenly encountered the pilot, who was carrying a revolver, and Harada, with a shotgun. Beni Kanahele was a man of great strength, said to be able to hoist three 150-pound (68-kilogram) honey cartons at once. He struggled with the pilot. When the flier got his gun arm free, Beni's wife rushed in and for a moment was able to keep him from shooting her husband, but Harada tackled the woman.

Beni, although shot in the stomach, refused to release the pilot. When shot again in the thigh he continued his bear hold. Then the pilot shot him once more. Telling his story later, Kanahele said, "Then I got mad!" He grabbed the pilot by his neck and one leg and smashed his head against a stone wall. Harada turned the gun on himself and committed suicide.

Mrs. Kanahele hurried to the village for help for Beni, but he finally grew tired of waiting and walked in himself for attention to his three wounds.

This memorable defense of American soil in World War II had come to a successful conclusion.

The strange course of that "Battle of Niihau" revealed much about the traditional wisdom, strength, bravery, and loyalty that have been so characteristic of the people of Hawaii over the years.

Lay of the Land

"ISLES OF EDEN"

"Hawaii rests like a water lily on the swelling bosom of the Pacific. The heaven is tranquil above our heads, and the sun keeps his jealous eye upon us every day while his rays are so tempered that they never wither prematurely what they have warmed into life."

That poetic description was given by a man who knew and loved the Hawaiian islands—Kamehameha IV, king of Hawaii. Almost everyone who ever set eyes on the islands—before or since—has been impressed. Mark Twain called them "the loveliest fleet of islands that lies anchored in any ocean." English travel writer Isabella Bird, who spent six months there in 1873, exclaimed: "It was a dream, a rapture.... These are indeed the 'Isles of Eden.'"

Even the geography of Hawaii calls for apparent exaggerations. It is the longest island chain in the world. The southernmost tip of the island of Hawaii is the most southerly point in the United States. From there to the tiny speck of land called Kure, the islands stretch for 1,600 miles (2,575 kilometers) from southeast to northwest.

There are about 130 islands altogether. Seven of these are inhabited and five are considered major—Hawaii, Maui, Oahu, Kauai, and Molokai, in order of size.

Geographically, Hawaii is said by some to have "one of the world's most fortunate locations." Not only is the climate unsurpassed, but the location gives the islands importance as the gateway to the Orient and the South Seas. Honolulu is 2,397 miles (3,858 kilometers) from San Francisco; the nearest inhabited land west of Niihau, except for such fortified islets as Wake and Johnston, is Guam, almost 3,000 miles (4,830 kilometers) away. In these vast distances, the very fact that Hawaii is there makes it truly master of the Pacific.

BORN IN FURY

Millions of years ago a great 2,000-mile (3,200-kilometer) long

11

fault (or crack) opened in the floor of the Pacific Ocean. In the underwater cataclysms that followed, the Hawaiian Islands were spewed up from the bottom of the sea. They were built up by untold billions of tons of basaltic lava rushing from the molten depths of the earth.

In addition to the accumulation of lava, the islands also have been pushed higher by a general raising of the surface. We know this by examining areas such as the shoreline of Lanai, where fossils once in the sea are now raised to heights up to 1,000 feet (305 meters).

The first major island to emerge from these building processes was Kauai, considered the oldest of the islands with an age of about ten million years. The largest island, Hawaii, is the youngest, and the volcanic action that created these lands is still occurring. Here is the world's most impressive geography lesson, showing plainly that the work of these volcanoes is architecture — not destruction.

At present the builder is the magnificent Mauna Loa volcano, the world's most active volcano and the greatest creator of new land. In the great eruption of Mauna Loa in 1855, lava covered 12.2 square miles (31.6 square kilometers) of Hawaii. In 1859, the flow added an entire new promontory to the island's seacost. The flow in 1880 and 1881 covered an area of some 24 square miles (62 square kilometers). Lava from more recent flows, particularly 1950, which covered 35.6 square miles (92 square kilometers), is still hot.

The following eyewitness description of the eruption of 1868 is one of the most graphic: "The ground south of Hilo burst open with a crash and roar.... A molten river ... emerged through a fissure two miles in length with tremendous force and volume. It was in a pleasant pastoral region supposed to be at rest forever, at the top of a grass-covered plateau sprinkled with native and foreign houses, and rich in herds of cattle.

"Four huge fountains boiled up with terrific fury, throwing crimson lava and rocks weighing many tons to a height from 500 to 1,000 feet.... From these great fountains flowed a rapid stream of red lava, rolling, rushing and tumbling like a swollen river ... surging and roaring throughout its length like a cataract with a power and fury perfectly indescribable.

12

The lava fountains that fascinated Isabella Bird in 1837 continue to be active today in Kilauea Crater at Hawaii Volcanoes National Park.

"It was nothing less than a river of fire from 200 to 800 feet wide and twenty deep, with a speed varying from ten to twenty-five miles an hour.... Where it entered the sea it extended the coast-line half a mile.... Though the region was very thinly peopled, 200 houses and 100 lives were sacrificed in this week of horrors.... The number of shocks of earthquake counted was 2,000 in two weeks."

Down the slope of Mauna Loa, the crater of Kilauea is intermittently active, giving its fire pit the name House of Everlasting Fire or the Fiery Pit.

On a visit in 1873, Isabella Bird described Kilauea: "Suddenly we stood on the brink.... I think we all screamed.... It is the most unutterable of wonderful things.... On our arrival eleven fire fountains were playing joyously ... it was all confusion, commotion, force, terror, glory, majesty, mystery.... Had I not seen it I would not have known that such crimson color was possible.... The beauty of these jets made a profound impression upon me, and the sight of them must always remain one of the most fascinating recollections of my life.''

With such activity continuing over millions of years it is not surprising that Mauna Loa has grown to be what is considered the largest single mountain mass in the world. It is about 32,000 feet (9,754 meters) high, including the 18,000-foot (5,486-meter) portion below sea level and the 13,680 feet (4,170 meters) that can be seen. The extent of its mighty base, far in the depths of the ocean, is only an estimate.

The island of Hawaii was built by five volcanoes, all inactive now except for Mauna Loa and its vent, Kilauea. The tallest of these is majestic Mauna Kea, the highest point in Hawaii at 13,796 feet (4,205 meters).

The Crater of Kilauea on Hawaii Island as painted by Titian R. Peale.

The inside of Haleakala Crater, Maui, is so large that the entire city of New York could fit inside.

The islands have numerous reminders of the volcanoes that created them. Two huge volcanoes, Eke and Haleakala, formed the island of Maui. These are linked by an isthmus. Haleakala has the largest inactive volcanic crater complex in the world. The inside is so enormous that the entire city of New York could be swallowed up within it and not leave a trace.

Even Honolulu lies in the remains of the ancient volcanic craters. One of the world's best-known landmarks, Diamond Head, off Waikiki, is also a volcanic crater. Here, according to legend, lived the mighty goddess Pele, who controlled all volcanoes. Other Oahu landmarks are Koko Head, Koko Crater, and Punchbowl.

In places experiencing recent lava flows, there is only desolation, such as the barren lava deserts on Hawaii. Some lava-covered regions make the visitor feel as if he or she were walking across the craters of the moon. Much of the lava is in the rough form called 'a 'a by the Hawaiians. Stranger still is the threadlike lava known as "Pele's hair." This looks like a coarse spun glass. Some of the lava,

15

called *pahoehoe,* covers large areas in waves like the ocean, some black, others iridescent. Certain lava remnants twist in loops and folds like giant serpents or tree roots.

Where the flows are older, wind and rain have begun to erode and break down the lava into the rich Hawaiian soil. The razor edges have been softened, and valley floors have been filled and flattened with fertile volcanic soil ground down by the forces of nature. These valleys account for the most fertile level land in the state.

The Koolau Mountains form a backdrop for Honolulu. In the western part of Oahu are the Waianae Mountains, with Mount Kaala the highest point on the island, at 4,025 feet (1,227 meters).

CLIMATE THAT SWEETENS ONE'S BONES

It is frequently written that the Hawaiian language has no word for weather. Apparently there was no reason for mentioning something that was so perfect and unvarying. As Robert Louis Stevenson said, "The climate sweetens one's bones."

Hawaii is the only tropical state in the United States. This is not to say that the climate is the same on all parts of the islands. In fact, the opposite is true; there is great variety of climate, but in any given place the seasonal changes are slight. The monthly mean temperature at Honolulu varies from 70° F. (21.1° C.) in February to 78° F. (25.6° C.) in August. Those who live in Hawaii can take their choice of the tropical weather at sea level or go up into the higher lands. The mercury drops about four degrees for every 1,000 feet (305 meters) of ascent. In some places there is frost every night, and residents sleep under blankets. The summits of Mauna Loa and Mauna Kea are snowcapped during the winter months.

The northeast trade winds blow most of the time, but in the winter they can be interrupted by variable or southwest winds, called *Konas,* that bring rain and high humidity. These last from a few hours to two or three days.

The amount and the variations in rainfall are both fantastic. Mount Waialeale on Kauai is known as the wettest place on earth, with an average annual rainfall of 472 inches (about 1,200 centimeters) and a high of 624 inches (1,585 centimeters) in 1948. In 1956 Kilauea, Kauai, had 45 inches (114 centimeters) of rain within thirty-six hours. Yet in the driest parts of the state only about 8 inches (20 centimeters) of rain falls in a year. The tremendous difference occurs because the rains are dropped on the windward sides of the islands. On the leeward sides, away from the wind, the climate is generally arid. Many Hawaiians insist that it often rains on one side of a street and not on the other.

RUSHING WATERS

In spite of the huge rainfall, Hawaii has the least inland water of any of the states—only nine square miles (twenty-three square kilometers). This is because the sloping nature of the land provides almost no place for water to collect in the form of lakes. During the years, the rainwater rushing down to the ocean has cut hundreds— even thousands—of small valleys into the mountain slopes.

These parallel valleys are responsible for the strange wrinkled appearance of the islands' surfaces as seen on relief maps. Probably no other place on earth has a similar landscape. Typical of this strange, rugged, and beautiful land structure is the section of coast between Hilo and Laupahoehoe. Here sixty-five streams are found within a distance of thirty miles (forty-eight kilometers), each one cutting a new crease on its way to the sea.

Watercourses on the islands do not generally qualify to be called rivers but, rather, streams. The only navigable rivers in the state are on Kauai. Principal rivers on Kauai are the Hanapepe and Wailua. For the most part the rivers of Kauai are fed by the unique Alakai Swamp, a thirty-square-mile (seventy-eight-square-kilometer) morass that collects and distributes the huge amount of rainfall on Mount Waialeale.

Carved by the great rainfall, the gorges on Kauai are Hawaii's deepest and widest, and are said by some to be "unique on the face of the earth." The Waimea ("red water") River is the chief carver

Waimea Canyon on Kauai is known as the Grand Canyon of Hawaii.

of the Waimea Canyon—known as the Grand Canyon of Hawaii. Its colors are said by some to be even more beautiful than those of the much larger one in Arizona. Waimea Canyon is 2,857 feet (871 meters) deep, a mile (1.6 kilometers) wide, and 10 miles (16 kilometers) long.

Kalalau Valley, as seen from the 4,000-foot (1,220-meter) height of Kalalau Lookout, has been called the eighth wonder of Hawaii by author James Michener. This view is one of the most spectacular in the world.

Because of the heavy rainfall and stony heights, Hawaii contains numerous intermittent waterfalls. After heavy rains, cascades leap over countless bluffs and crevices. Akaka Falls on the island of Hawaii plunges 420 feet (128 meters) in a shimmering veil. Hanapepe Falls on Kauai is another of the better-known water drops.

Among the few lakes of the state now accessible by auto is Lake Waiau, near the top of Mauna Kea at the 13,020-foot (3,968-meter) level. It is the highest lake in the United States.

18

Footsteps on the Land

DAYS OF THE MENEHUNE

For twenty-five miles (forty kilometers) there stretched a continuous double line of Menehune, the legendary 3-foot (91-centimeter) tall people of Hawaii. According to legend, along this line all through the night the Menehune passed building blocks, hand-to-hand, from the Makaweli quarry to the banks of Huleia Stream on Kauai. By morning a 900-foot (274-meter) dam of precisely fitted blocks had been built, a 4-foot (1.2-meter) wide wall reaching above the water for 5 feet (1.5 meters)—a wonderful feat of Stone Age engineers.

Legend says the job was done for a prince and princess who were forbidden to watch the work. When the Menehune discovered the royal couple watching them, they had the pair turned into stone. A local story claims that this accounts for the two strange pillars of rock near the Alekoko Fish Pond.

The story is pure fancy, but the stone dam creating the fish pond is not. It rests there as firmly today as when it was built. Another fitted-

Menehune Fish Pond, Kauai

stone construction is the Menehune Ditch, a prehistoric aqueduct on the Waimea River. More prehistoric stone remains found in various parts of the islands demonstrate the work and skill of the laborers under the leadership of their chiefs.

Whether or not the legend of the Menehune has any basis in fact, the stories about these little people are among the most interesting in all folklore. They are said to be the original Brownies. The Menehune were supposed to have done all their work at night. If they could not finish a project in one night, they simply abandoned it. Their wages consisted of fish or shrimp, and when they were paid in the morning and ate their feast with joyful celebration, the noise of their party could be heard from one island to another.

SEAFARERS OF ANTIQUITY

The great double-hulled canoes danced on the water. In each of these tough but fragile-looking craft, scores of people had been roaming the surface of the sea for countless anxious weeks. Suddenly the cry went up, " 'Aina!" (Land!). In the far distance a few jagged rock silhouettes had pierced the horizon. The Polynesians had found a new home—Hawaii.

Scientists are continuing to unravel the story of who these people were and where they came from. We do know that as many as a hundred could exist for weeks in one large double canoe. They brought their food and carried water in gourds, coconuts, or bamboo pipes with the ends plugged. The seamanship they used in navigating the vast Pacific was remarkable for the time.

Recent discoveries indicate that the Polynesians arrived at the islands we call Hawaii at a much earlier date than had been thought previously. It is now believed that they came as early as 500 A.D.— possibly from the Marquesas Islands. They brought with them evidences of Indo-Malay culture.

Once the long voyage had been made, some of the first arrivals returned home to bring more settlers to the new-found land. These voyages may have continued for many years.

Seafaring traditions are now "adapted" to create first-rate tourist attractions, as at the Polynesian Cultural Center.

During the centuries that followed, the descendants of those first pioneers created a civilization of considerable strength and culture.

Islands or portions of islands were ruled by hereditary chiefs or kings. It was not unusual for a woman to be a chief, though not a ruler. Priests and advisers held high places in the government. The common people obeyed their masters. However, they could search for a new chief if their master became too severe.

The Hawaiian people recognized four main gods: Kane, procreator, provider of sunlight, fresh air, and the life substances of nature; Ku, the god of war—the only one that demanded human sacrifices;

Lono, the god of peace, agriculture, and games; and Kanaloa, lord of the ocean and the ocean winds. More than a hundred minor gods and goddesses were part of the Hawaiian mythology. To secure the success of any enterprise, the proper god had to be made friendly by prayer, an offering, or even an elaborate ritual.

The people believed that many persons and things possessed certain powers—*mana*—for either good or evil. Because of this, some things and some people should be avoided as *kapu,* a term we know better as "tabu." Penalty for breaking a *kapu* was often death.

Priests directed the common people in building temples *(heiaus)* for their services of worship. In one type of *heiau* the sacrifices consisted of human beings, dogs, and hogs, first put to death, then placed on the altar. Remains of these ancient temples are found on all the major islands.

Hale-O-Keawe Heiau, *a temple at the City of Refuge National Historical Park.*

Hundreds of years ago Hawaiians were enjoying surfing, the ancient sport of all the people.

Other *heiaus* were built for entirely different purposes. They were places of refuge, and all who were hunted or oppressed, even criminals, were safe once they were inside the walls of these refuges. No warrior could pursue his victim beyond the gate of the temple of refuge. Women and children often waited there in safety during wartime.

The hula dance began as part of the ancient religious ceremonies. It was originally a sacred ritual in honor of the goddess Laka.

Modern civilization only recently has caught up with many of the practices of the Hawaiians. Hundreds of years ago island residents were swimming, sun bathing on the beaches, and enjoying the thrills of surfing. Surfing was the ancient sport of all the people. A sport of kings was summer tobogganing. Slides, sometimes a mile (1.6 kilometers) long, were constructed on the slopes. These were covered with dry grass and made slippery with kukui nut oil. Wooden sledges called *holua* were used for the swift descent.

Eating was a favorite pastime in Hawaii. Here the cookout originated, with wonderful feasts called *aha 'aina*. "Their ceremony of eating," according to A.P. Taylor, "was far superior to that prevailing in the baronial halls of Europe, where gluttony and lack of niceties in the partaking of food were in contrast to the delicacy of methods prevailing at the fern-covered tables of the chiefs under Hawaiian skies. Trunks of trees fashioned into bowls, beautifully polished, and other bowls of varying sizes and designs furnished the table.

"There were large, round bowls for poi, long, concave trenchers of roasted pig; wide flat ones for fish, small calabashes and gourds for relishes and desserts; large ones filled with water, with fern leaves floating upon the surface, for use as finger bowls—providing the ancient Hawaiian with dishes that, in a measure, are as beautiful as the chinaware which graces modern civilized tables.

"There was no hasty use of both hands over a fish, or fowl, or pig. Reclining upon one elbow, even as epicurean Romans and Greeks of old reclined, the chief used the fingers of the other hand to separate the flesh before him, and each morsel was conveyed to the lips with as much delicacy and grace of movement as possible, and the finger bowls were frequently used."

Calabashes were the most valuable household utensils. There were remarkable carved wooden bowls—some of them thirty inches (seventy-six centimeters) across. The prehistoric Hawaiians knew nothing about pottery; they had no metals or any kind of animal power, such as horses.

Fish for the royal table were propagated in man-made fish ponds, which were arms of the sea walled off by the people. Other ponds were used by the ancients as salt works, where sea water was evaporated for the mineral.

The islanders quarried the hardest basalt to make their tools. Some of these old quarries can be seen on the slopes of Mauna Loa. Partly finished tools lie on the ground as if the makers would be returning shortly.

24

Haughty Hawaiian warriors were skillful users of the spear, sling and stone, javelin, and war club. The famed Naha stone is now exhibited at the Hilo County Library. Special persons who could lift or move this huge stone qualified for consideration as king.

The ancient Hawaiians were skilled craftsmen in many fields, particularly in the use of feathers for cloaks and ornaments. The feather mantles of the Hawaiian kings must be ranked with the most beautiful and artistic garments ever created. Small forest birds furnished the red, yellow, and black feathers. Only the choicest feathers were used in making the kingly robes. Seven feathers were usually selected from the *mamo* birds. Glue was spread on trees to catch the birds or they were caught in nets. After the feathers were plucked, the birds were released.

During Aloha Week on Oahu, the ancient pageantry is recaptured.

The intricate process of making a feather cloak was begun by tying feathers together in twos or threes with twisted strands of the *olona*. These were woven into a foundation of netting made the same shape and size of the finished cloak. Sometimes these cloaks took a hundred years to make.

Symbol of the Hawaiian kings was the *kahili*, a cylinder of feathers. The handle or pole, traditionally of tortoise shell and human bone, supported a colorful and impressive cylinder of bird feathers. As many as seventy-six of these were said to have been carried in the funeral of one king. A feathered helmet was worn by the highest-ranking chief.

A clothlike material called *kapa* was made from the bark of paper mulberry trees. It was beaten and shaped in somewhat the same way as modern felt is made. *Kapa* garments often were decorated with artistic designs printed from bamboo "stamps" dipped in vegetable or mineral dyes. Women wore *kapa* skirts, and men and women both draped loose *kapa* capes across their shoulders in cool weather. The men wore loin cloths of *kapa*.

Most of the island inhabitants were fishermen or farmers. They paid taxes to the kings and chiefs in the form of fish, farm products, *kapa* sheets, fish nets, mats, and other handicrafts. The people loved their traditional music and song. Before Europeans came to the islands, there were very few health problems. Both men and women were vigorous and athletic. Men loved fishing, wrestling, boxing, and bowling. More than 150 games and pastimes were engaged in by the Hawaiian people.

Although the following description was written in 1873, the scene must have been quite the same for centuries in Hawaii before the Europeans came: "Here stands a native grass house, with passionflowers clustering round its veranda, and the great solitary, red blossoms of the hibiscus flame out from dark surrounding leafage, and women . . . weaving garlands, greet us with 'Aloha' as we pass."

Among the reminders of the early people in Hawaii are some of the most extensive petroglyphs found anywhere. These designs or messages carved into the rocks include the Luahiwa petroglyphs of Lanai and those of Olowalu, Maui, and several thousand in various

Petroglyphs such as these in Kona Village are among the reminders of the early people of Hawaii.

spots on Hawaii. As is true with such carvings all over the world, their meanings have been only partly interpreted.

GODS ON FLOATING ISLANDS

In 1778 the ancient lands of Hawaii experienced a most important event. The people were electrified to see two "floating islands" populated by strange-looking men. This was the exploring expedition of English Captain James Cook. Cook and his men first sighted the island of Oahu and made the first landing in Hawaii by Europeans on the island of Kauai at Waimea. Cook named the group the Sandwich Islands in honor of the Earl of Sandwich, who was his patron. Then he sailed on to explore other regions. One of the officers in Cook's party was William Bligh, who later lost his ship in the mutiny on the *Bounty*.

The Cook expedition returned to the Sandwich Islands, and in January 1779 sailed into Kealakekua Bay on the west coast of Hawaii

Early painting (above) depicts the Death of Captain Cook *in Hawaii.*
Below: The monument to Captain Cook on the island of Hawaii.

Island. Here, ten thousand Hawaiians came out to greet the ships. Cook himself described the scene: "Canoes now began to arrive from all parts . . . not fewer than a thousand about the two ships. . . . I had nowhere . . . seen so numerous a body of people assembled in one place . . . all the shore of the bay was covered with spectators, and many hundreds were swimming round the ships like shoals of fish."

The islanders hailed Cook as the returned great god Lono, the god of growing things. The spirit of *Aloha* was one of their strongest customs. Hawaiians felt it was their sacred obligation to welcome strangers with the greatest possible generosity and kindness, and so they took Cook and his men to their hearts.

Despite this kindness, Cook ordered part of the temple and its fence torn down for firewood, and the expedition left a legacy of disease that has continued to the present time. The Hawaiians were so eager to obtain nails, the first metal they had ever seen, that for one nail they would exchange enough food to feed a ship's crew for a whole day. In this way Cook's men depleted the Kona section of the island of most of its produce, chickens, and hogs, which the islanders were glad to give for bits of metal.

Amply stocked with provisions, Cook and his men sailed away. But when a storm broke the mast of his ship *Resolution,* they returned to Kealakekua and found a different welcome. The islanders had thought about Cook's many injustices; they began to steal the coveted iron, even burning one of the small boats to get the nails.

Unwisely, Cook tried to capture some local leaders as hostages to exchange for some of the stolen merchandise. A crowd of warriors began to congregate. Cook abandoned his threat to take prisoners and started for his boat, but one of his men fired a gun, and a fight began. During the struggle Cook was struck with a club. When he groaned the Hawaiians were astounded; no real god would groan. Several vengeful Hawaiians descended on the captain, stabbing him to death. His body was taken to the temple, where it was prepared for burial in the manner reserved for Hawaiian chiefs, that is by stripping the flesh from the bones.

After a week of fighting in which six Hawaiian chiefs were also killed, the Hawaiians returned the remaining parts of Cook's body to his men. They buried their captain in the bay with full naval honors. The black lava rock on which tradition says the captain met his end may still be seen at Kealakekua Bay.

NAPOLEON OF THE PACIFIC

One of the chiefs who had visited on board Cook's ships and took part in the fighting against Cook's men was a vigorous young warrior named Kamehameha. He was impressed with much of the Europeans' organization, discipline, and weapons. Kamehameha gradually gathered a group of loyal followers, and in a series of battles, Kamehameha began to consolidate his power on his native island of Hawaii.

One of the most successful in opposing Kamehameha was high chief Keoua. Although Kamehameha had not been able to defeat the armies of Keoua, the forces of nature came to his aid. When the forces of Keoua were moving across the island, an explosive eruption of the Kilauea volcano occurred. An entire wing of Keoua's army was killed, along with the wives and children who were accompanying them. On what is now called Footprints Trail in Hawaii Volcanoes National Park, one can still see the footprints of some of those soldiers in the hardened volcanic ash.

About a year after the eruption, Kamehameha sent two of his most trusted chiefs to Chief Keoua, risking the danger of his enemy's wrath. They brought an invitation from Kamehameha for Keoua to take part in ceremonies dedicating *Puu Kohola* Temple. Kamehameha had decided that only the sacrifice of a very high chief would be suitable for such a ceremony, although, of course, this was not made known to Keoua.

However, it is thought that Chief Keoua must have known that Kamehameha would murder him. He may have believed that the earlier destruction of his army by the volcano was a sign that the goddess Pele wished him to sacrifice his life. In any event, Chief Keoua arrived for the ceremonies in a great canoe, accompanied by his honor guard. He wore a magnificent feather cloak and helmet. Kamehameha, dressed even more magnificently, stood on the shore to welcome him. Just as King Keoua called out a greeting, Keeaumoku, one of Kamehameha's close advisors, stabbed Chief Keoua with his spear.

With Keoua's death, the last strong opposition to Kamehameha on the island of Hawaii vanished, and Kamehameha was the master of the Big Island.

Then Kamehameha put in motion a plan that none of the other kings or chiefs of the islands had dared—possibly none of them had ever thought of it. He set out to conquer all of the Hawaiian Islands.

In beautiful, usually peaceful, Iao Valley on Maui, an historic battle was fought. Kamehameha's forces had forced back the warriors of Maui. Unable to escape up the steep valley walls, the Maui troops were trapped and killed in fearful numbers. So many died that Iao Stream in the valley was completely dammed with the bodies, backing up the water that ran red with blood. This 1790 slaughter has been called the Battle of Kepaniwai, the Hawaiian word meaning "damming of the waters." Kamehameha now ruled both Hawaii and Maui.

In 1795 the great war fleets of Kamehameha's canoes pushed ashore at Waialae and Waikiki to begin their invasion of Oahu. Until

Memories of the great invasion fleet still linger in the islands.

this time Oahu had remained under the control of Chief Kalanikupule. The chief and his men put up a brave struggle, but slowly they were forced to retreat up the beautiful Nuuanu Valley. At last they came to the awful brink at the end of the valley—Nuuanu Pali. (Pali is the Hawaiian term for cliff or precipice.)

A few of the defeated Oahu warriors found their way down the cliff's cracks and crevices. Many were killed or captured. Most of Oahu's brave army were forced over the edge of the precipice and dashed to their death on the jagged rocks below. For years their skeletons lay bleaching in the sun where they had fallen. Chief Kalanikupule managed to escape, but after wandering through the Koolau Mountains for many weeks, he was finally captured and offered as a sacrifice to Kukailimoku, the war god of Kamehameha.

In this Battle of Nuuanu, Kamehameha had become the undisputed master of the Hawaiian archipelago. Only the islands of Niihau and Kauai were not under his direct rule. But King Kaumualii of Kauai paid tribute to King Kamehameha, and after Kamehameha's death those islands joined the Hawaiian kingdom. In his lifetime King Kamehameha I had many extraordinary achievements. A more detailed and personal account of Kamehameha, who became known as the Napoleon of the Pacific, is given in a later section. King Kamehameha the Great died in 1819, leaving the kingdom of Hawaii as a legacy for his descendants.

THE ROYAL DYNASTY

During the period of Kamehameha the Great, foreigners began to come to the islands. Some had great influence with the king. Two Britishers, Isaac Davis and John Young, became highly regarded advisers. Explorer Captain George Vancouver made three visits between 1792 and 1795. He introduced cattle and sheep from California into the Hawaiian Islands. The first American to enter Honolulu harbor was a Captain Brown, who put in for repairs to his whaling vessel in 1794.

In the early years of the reign of Kamehameha I, the capital had been the sleepy town of Lahaina on Maui. He moved the seat of government and his royal court to Waikiki in 1804. Taking over the throne on the death of his father was twenty-three-year-old Prince Liholiho, who became Kamehameha II.

The islanders were still steeped in the customs of *Kapu* and worship of gods who called for human sacrifices. Kamehameha II, his mother, Queen Keopuolani, and Queen Kaahumanu, another widow of Kamehameha I, determined to end these practices. With great courage, the king ate with the women in defiance of the prevailing beliefs. He proclaimed that the old religion was dead. Thus the people, especially the women, were relieved of much hardship and discrimination.

King Kamehameha II and his queen made the long voyage to London in 1824 to see for themselves how people in more highly developed areas of the world lived. The people of England received them with great enthusiasm. Sadly, however, they both caught measles and died within a few days of one another. Their bodies were carried back to Hawaii with much ceremony on the British frigate *Blonde.*

Another son of Kamehameha the Great, Kauikeaouli, was proclaimed king, with the title of Kamehameha III. During his remarkable thirty-year reign, the little kingdom survived many crises and made considerable progress. The feudal system was gradually transformed into a constitutional monarchy, with a constitution being proclaimed in 1840.

In a strange turn of events in 1843, British Lord George Paulet forced the Hawaiian kingdom to place itself under his rule. It appeared that Hawaii might now be like the rest of the countries in the British Empire. However, after only five months, British Rear Admiral Richard Thomas repudiated Lord Paulet's action and restored the kingdom to Kamehameha III.

At that time King Kamehameha made his memorable statement, *"Ua mau ke ea o ka aina i ka pono,"* which means, "The life of the land is perpetuated in righteousness." This has become the motto of Hawaii. Later, Britain, France, and the United States all recognized Hawaii's independence.

King Kamehameha III died in 1854; his nephew, Alexander Liholiho, grandson of Kamehameha the Great, became King Kamehameha IV. The little prince, Kamehameha IV's son, was especially beloved. Queen Victoria of England was his godmother. However, he died at the age of four. Kamehameha IV ruled for nine years and, because he had no heir, he was succeeded by his brother, Lot Kamehameha, known as Kamehameha V. When he died in 1872, the direct line of succession of Kamehameha the Great ended.

The almost eighty-year period of the Kamehameha dynasty saw an overwhelming transformation of the Hawaiian Islands. Sugar plantations were established and the first imported laborers were brought in. A new constitution in 1852 established a bicameral legislature (two houses) and set up courts of law. Honolulu was declared a city, the capital of the kingdom in 1850, and a public water system was installed.

At one time, only royalty could own property. Private property rights were recognized in 1848, and royal lands were divided. This division was known as The Great Mahele. Other changes and the progress made in business, industry, and agriculture are taken up in later sections.

"E ALA NA MOKU KAI LILOLOA"

Probably the most important and far-reaching of all the many changes in Hawaiian life involved the coming of Christianity.

The beginning of this development took place, oddly enough, in faraway Connecticut. In 1808 a sixteen-year-old Hawaiian boy named Opukahaia had swum out to an American ship anchored in Kealakekua Bay and begged the captain to take him to the United States. He was being trained to be a priest by his uncle, who was also a priest. However, Opukahaia had seen his parents killed in one of the tribal wars. He hated the fierce island religion and the bloodshed and wanted to leave Hawaii. So he became the cabin boy of Captain Brintnal of New Haven, Connecticut.

Brintnal took Opukahaia with him to New Haven, and the story is told that one evening Opukahaia was found weeping on the steps of Yale University because he could not receive an education there. Professor Edwin W. Dwight of Yale took him into his home. Traveling throughout New England, Opukahaia spoke so eloquently on the need for missionaries in his homeland that the Reverend Samuel Mills established a pioneer school at Cornwall, Connecticut, for the training of people for missionary work.

Opukahaia, who had been given the first name of Henry, became the star pupil of the school, but his dream of bringing Christianity to Hawaii was never realized; he died of typhus in 1818. However, he had inspired others with the same dream, and on October 23, 1819, seventeen Congregational missionaries led by the Reverend Hiram Bingham and the Reverend Asa Thurston sailed from Boston for the Sandwich Islands.

The first missionaries arrived at Kailua, Kona, on Hawaii Island in April 1820, on board the *Thaddeus*. It has been said that "America had its *Mayflower* and Hawaii its *Thaddeus*—the spiritual ideals of a nation were brought by both."

The missionaries had been commissioned not only to convert the people of Hawaii but to bring advancements of civilization. In the beginning the missionaries could not even communicate with the Hawaiians, and there was no written language. However, the missionaries learned the language, created an alphabet, and translated the Bible. They brought in skilled printers and a press, and by 1839 the entire Bible was in print in Hawaiian.

Most of the missionaries were teachers as well as religious leaders, and schools sprang up from Hanalei on Kauai to Puna on Hawaii. In an incredibly short time the islands had one of the highest literacy rates on earth. Within twenty-six years after the first missionaries arrived, 80 percent of the people could read and write. Women learned nursing, hat and mat weaving, dressmaking, and homemaking in addition to the three Rs. Mission doctors traveled almost constantly to bring better health to the people.

When the old religion was first abolished, the people had nothing to take its place, but still the missionaries had little success for some years in converting the people to Christianity. However, there were

*The early missionaries
built houses such
as these in Hawaii.*

some early successes, including the conversion of the Chiefess Kapiolani. In 1825 the chiefess announced that she would defy the goddess Pele. Ignoring the pleadings of her husband and friends and leading a procession of fearful followers, Chiefess Kapiolani marched 100 miles (161 kilometers), mostly on foot and over rugged lava, to the crater Kilauea. She ate the sacred *ohelo* berries and defied the goddess to punish her. When Kapiolani and her frightened followers returned unharmed it was a great triumph for Christianity.

In spite of such individual successes, the number of conversions remained small until 1837. Then all over the islands whole villages gathered at mission stations. The population of Hilo swelled from one thousand to ten thousand. The blowing of a conch shell might bring together as many as a thousand worshippers. For almost two years the people studied the new morality, and great numbers were then baptized.

The first Roman Catholic missionaries arrived in 1839 and the first Mormon missionaries in 1850. Other denominations joined the work at various times.

Christianity was proclaimed the national religion by Kamehameha III. However, complete religious tolerance was guaranteed.

36

The nineteenth-century missionaries made many notable contributions to the Hawaiian Islands. In later years, their work has often been downgraded and their motives questioned. However, others would agree with writer Richard H. Dana when he said, "It is no small thing to say of the missionaries of the American Board, that in less than forty years they have taught this whole people to read and to write, to cipher and to sew. They have given them an alphabet, grammar, and dictionary; preserved their language from extinction; given it a literature, and translated into it the Bible and works of devotion, science, and entertainment, etc.

"They have established schools, reared up native teachers and so pressed their work that now the proportion of inhabitants who can read and write is greater than in New England. And whereas they found these islanders a nation of half-naked savages, living in the surf and on the sand, eating raw fish, fighting among themselves, tyrannized over by feudal chiefs, and abandoned to sensuality, they now see them decently clothed, recognizing the law of marriage, knowing something of accounts, going to school and public worship more regularly than the people do at home, and the more elevated of them taking part in conducting the affairs of the constitutional monarchy under which they live."

One of the best illustrations of the missionaries' success was the fact that by 1852 the people of Hawaii were already sending missionaries to other island groups, such as the Carolines, Gilberts, and Marshalls.

As Gilbert Grosvenor said about the missionaries, "They saved the Hawaiian race from such ravages of disease and ignorance as decimated the islanders of the South Pacific. They hitched Hawaii's wagon to a star. They pointed the way which their descendants and the thousands of splendid men and women who have since made the Hawaiian Islands their home have zealously followed. It was their children and grandchildren who guided the successive sovereigns of Hawaii in preventing its absorption by European powers, and who, when the islanders had outgrown the monarch, led the movement for independence, and ultimate entrance of Hawaii as an integral part of the United States."

Although Henry Opukahaia never returned to his native land, it followed his dying command, *"E ala na moku kai liloloa!"* which means "Awaken, ye islands of the faraway sea!"

MORE MERRY MONARCHS

With the death of Kamehameha V, there was no legal heir to the throne. The legislature elected Prince William C. Lunalilo to be king. He died a year later, and the legislature again chose a monarch—this time David Kalakaua. Dowager Queen Emma, widow of Kamehameha IV, had hoped to be chosen as the ruler, and there was a period of civil disturbance. King Kalakaua was forced to call on American and British marines, who were in Hawaii, to restore order.

King Kalakaua, known as the Merry Monarch, battled constantly to gain more personal power for the king. He made a trip around the world and dreamed of founding a mighty empire of all the Polynesian lands.

World traveler Isabella Bird, who spent six months in Hawaii during Lunalilo's brief reign, had many fascinating things to tell about what life was like in Hawaii in those days. She wrote: "This is a blessed country, for a lady can travel everywhere in absolute security. . . . There is not a locked door in Hilo, and nobody makes anybody else afraid. . . . I never saw such healthy bright complexions as among the women or such sparkling smiles. . . . Men and women looked as easy, contented, and happy as if care never came near them. . . . The people live more happily than any that I have seen elsewhere. It is pleasant to be among people whose faces are not soured. . . .

"The beach and the pleasant lawn above it are always covered with men and women riding at a gallop, with bare feet, and stirrups tucked between the toes. To walk even 200 yards seems considered a degradation. The people meet outside each other's houses all day long, and sit in picturesque groups on their mats, singing, laughing, talking. . . . Pleasant sights of outdoor cooking are carried on everywhere. . . . A hole in the ground is lined with stones, wood is burned within it, and when the rude oven has been sufficiently heated, the pig, chicken, breadfruit, or kalo wrapped in ti leaves, is put in, a little water is thrown on, and the hole is covered up. It is a slow but sure process. . . .

"The dwindling of the race is a most pathetic subject. If the decrease is not arrested, in a quarter of a century, there will not be an Hawaiian left. The chiefs, or ali'i, are a nearly extinct order; and with few exceptions, those who remain are childless. In riding through Hawaii I came everywhere upon traces of a once numerous population where the hill slopes are now only a wilderness, upon churches and schoolhouses all too large, while in some hamlets the voices of children are altogether wanting.

"Population at Captain Cook's time may have been 300,000 in 1779. In 1872 it was only 49,000. It is a pity the race is dying out. It has shown a singular aptitude for politics and civilization.

"The hotel [in Honolulu] was lately built by the government at a cost of $120,000. . . . This is the perfection of a hotel. Hospitality seems to take possession as soon as one enters its never-closed door. . . . One can sit all day on the back verandah, watching the play of light and color on the mountains and Nuuanu Valley, where showers, sunshine, and rainbows make perpetual variety. . . . In the great dining room piles of bananas, guavas, limes, and oranges decorate the tables. . . . The host is German, the manager American, steward Hawaiian, and servants all Chinese men. . . . The charges are $3 a day, $15 a week.

"I went to a party given by Dowager Queen Emma . . . who received simply dressed in black silk. . . . The King stood on another lawn where presentations were made by the chamberlain. . . . He was dressed in a well-made black morning suit . . . but the display of gold lace of his staff was prodigious. . . . The chiefs are so raised above the common people in height, size, and general nobility of aspect, that many have supposed them to be of a different race, and the ali'i who represented the dwindled order of chiefs that night were certainly superb enough in appearance to justify the supposition. Beside their splendor and stateliness, the English and American officers in full-dress uniform looked decidedly insignificant.

"Chairs and benches were placed under the beautiful trees, and people flirted, talked politics and gossiped, or listened to the royal band, which played at intervals and played well.... The dress of the ladies ... was both pretty and appropriate.... Tea and ices were handed round on Sevres china by footmen and pages in liveries.... What a wonderful leap from calabashes and *poi, malos* and *paus,* to this correct and tasteful civilization!"

King Kalakaua had many ties with the United States. He became the first reigning monarch of any nation to visit the United States. He promoted a trade agreement in 1875 providing an American market for Hawaiian sugar. In 1887 the United States was given treaty rights to a naval coaling station on Oahu.

King Kalakaua died during a trip to San Francisco in 1891. He was succeeded by his sister, who became Queen Liliuokalani. She wanted to restore the absolute power of the monarch and tried to set up a new constitution giving herself greatly increased power.

After reigning only two years, Queen Liliuokalani, the last of the Hawaiian monarchs, was overthrown in a bloodless revolution in 1893. A temporary republic was set up, with Sanford Ballard Dole as first president. Dole and his other American supporters hoped that the United States would take over the islands, but President Grover Cleveland opposed this measure.

However, after the Spanish-American War, American opinion changed. The tremendous value of the islands to the United States defense system had become apparent. Under President William McKinley, on August 12, 1898, the Hawaiian Islands officially transferred sovereignty to the United States. Those who claim this was high-handed overlook the fact that this was a matter neither of purchase nor conquest. The changeover was carried out by a treaty accepted by both sides.

In 1900 Hawaii became a territory of the United States with Dole as first governor, and all of its residents became United States citizens.

Opposite: The beautiful Royal Coconut Grove on Kauai looks as if it could have been the setting for the party attended by world traveler Isabella Bird.

*Diamond Head Crater, the extinct volcano in
the background, is a landmark of Honolulu.*

Yesterday and Today

The progress of Hawaii from a chain of islands governed independently of each other, through periods as a kingdom, constitutional monarchy, independent republic, United States territory, and finally state, is unique in our history. Both Texas and California were once independent republics, but no other state was ever an independent monarchy, ruled by a king or queen. No other reigning emperors or kings ever resided in the United States.

When the territory of Hawaii was organized, the islands began earnest preparations for the last step in the progression. As early as 1903, Hawaii made a bid for statehood, but this was still to be far in the future.

In 1903 Hawaii's first pineapple was packed for commercial use; the islands' commerce and industry grew steadily, and a continual stream of laborers was brought in. This is taken up in more detail in later sections.

Hawaiians took part in World War I, but the territory itself played a relatively minor part in that conflict. The Hawaiian Homes Act of 1921 provided forty-acre (sixteen-hectare) farm and home sites on the island of Molokai for families of 50 percent or more Hawaiian blood. This was an effort to return the Hawaiian people to the land.

An important event occurred in 1927 when U.S. Army Lieutenants Lester Maitland and Albert Hegenberger made the first successful flight from the mainland. Air transportation would later transform the age-old relationships of the islands with the rest of the world.

The Great Depression of the 1930s did not affect Hawaii as seriously as other parts of the nation, because the islands did not depend so completely on industry. With growing world disputes and tensions, the American military buildup in Hawaii advanced to huge proportions. This brought a kind of prosperity based on government spending. Radio-telephone service placed the islands in instant communication with the rest of the world in 1931, and Franklin Delano Roosevelt in 1934 became the first United States president to visit Hawaii.

The coming of Pan American Airlines' regular passenger service between Hawaii and the mainland in 1936 brought the once-remote lands to within a few hours of the rest of the country.

"A DATE WHICH WILL LIVE IN INFAMY"

No one who awoke that peaceful morning of December 7, 1941, could have known that neither Hawaii nor the world would ever be the same again. The Catholic members of a United States cruiser at anchor in Pearl Harbor were just leaving for mass. Others were about their regular Sunday morning tasks. When a radar operator picked up some blips on his screen, he thought only that they indicated American planes he had been expecting.

As early as November 27, the commanders at Pearl Harbor had been warned of a possible attack, but nothing was done. Planes on the ground were not scattered widely apart for safety; few long range reconnaissance planes were sent out; ships in battleship row did not put out to sea but remained together, providing perfect targets.

No one knew then that six Japanese aircraft carriers and accompanying vessels had been on their way across the Pacific since November 26.

Suddenly, on the morning of December 7, at exactly 7:55 A.M., the public-address system of the battleship *Oklahoma* screamed, "Real planes, real bombs. This is no drill!" Japanese bombers began dropping high explosives, and fighter planes started to strafe airports, ships, and other vital targets.

After a second wave of planes had done its deadly work, the toll was 8 battleships and 3 cruisers either sunk or badly damaged, and 346 planes destroyed, most of them on the ground. A total of 2,403 Americans were killed and 1,178 wounded.

Except for the fact that several American aircraft carriers were away from the harbor on exercises, the disaster might have been far worse.

The next day President Roosevelt sternly told Congress that "Yesterday, December 7, 1941—a date which will live in infamy—

the United States of America was suddenly and deliberately attacked. . . '' He asked for and received a declaration of war against Japan.

Fighting did not return to Hawaiian shores except in isolated cases. One instance occurred on December 31, 1941, when a Japanese submarine reached close enough to Kauai to lob a direct hit on a gasoline storage tank there. Luckily it was a dud and did not go off.

As the war continued in the Pacific, Hawaii became the principal fortress of the war. Never before in the history of the world had such tremendous resources and strength been concentrated in such a small area. Hawaii contributed a full share of fighting men and employed the rest in agriculture and defense programs. Hawaii lived up to its promise of being the most important outpost in the world.

The war with Japan placed Hawaii's Americans of Japanese ancestry (AJAs) in an awkward position. Some people believed that the Japanese-Americans would be so bound by their ancient traditions and religion that they would be unable to take an active part in the war effort. However, these doubters were proven wrong. The Japanese responded magnificently and formed two outstanding military units. The ten thousand men in the 442nd Combat Infantry Team and the three thousand men in the 100th Infantry Battalion consisted largely of Nisei (second-generation Americans of Japanese ancestry) from Hawaii. The two groups united and fought in North Africa and Europe. They became the most decorated outfit of the entire war, if not in all American history. Their feats are said to be ''legendary.''

During the Korean War, which began in 1950, Hawaii provided more troops since it was closer to the scene of fighting. It had the tragic distinction of suffering more military casualties per capita than any other part of the country.

Another type of devastation—volcanic—occurred in 1950. Mauna Loa erupted in June and provided an awesome spectacle of twenty-three days of continuous activity. It was the largest eruption of historic times, as 615 million cubic yards (470 million cubic meters) of lava belched forth.

In 1955 and 1959 a cleft in Kilauea, dormant for more than a hundred years, suddenly burst open and covered more than six square miles (sixteen square kilometers) of land in the Puna area, including the favorite Warm Springs. Whenever such a spectacular eruption occurs, people from all over the islands and many parts of the world hurry to observe it, flying over in planes and approaching as close as possible on land.

Even more spectacular than the volcanoes, however, was the all-important event of 1959, an event that some citizens of Hawaii had been waiting and working for for almost sixty years. Actually, the first proposal for statehood had been made during the reign of Kamehameha III. At last, on March 12, 1959, President Dwight D. Eisenhower signed the proclamation making Hawaii the fiftieth state of the United States. The celebrations in Hawaii were almost unparalleled. On the Fourth of July, 1960, the first fifty-star flag was flung to the breezes. Oren E. Long and Hiram L. Fong were the first United States senators, Daniel K. Inoyue the first congressman, and William J. Quinn the first governor.

In 1960 Hawaii was hit by a tsunami (popularly known as a tidal wave). Hardest hit was Hilo, where sixty-one people lost their lives, and property damage was a horrible $50 million. The people of Hilo have rebuilt their city on higher and safer ground.

Hawaii kept pace with the jet age by opening the great Honolulu International Airport in 1961. That same year Hawaii became the first state to develop a comprehensive general plan for the rapid and orderly development of all aspects of the state's growth.

The 1970s have seen Hawaii's population increase at one of the fastest rates of any of the states. With this increase has come a growing concern for the environment and retention of the beauty and usefulness of the land. In 1974 the first governor of Japanese descent was inaugurated.

In another important field, the tourist boom vastly increased, emphasizing the state's importance as one of the world's premiere tourist centers.

Opposite: The tourist boom has brought visitors from all over the world to Hawaii's exotic shops.

THE PEOPLE OF HAWAII

Someone has said "the most fascinating scenery of the Hawaiian Islands is the people."

When the Hawaiian people began to decrease in number and the sugarcane fields required more labor, the first Chinese came to Hawaii in 1852. In the year 1868 alone, 140,000 Japanese laborers arrived in the islands to work the cane fields. Filipinos, Koreans, Portuguese, and Puerto Ricans all arrived in numbers.

Today there is a racial mixture in which no race has anything near a majority. According to the 1980 census, Caucasians of European ancestry make up about 40 percent of the population; Japanese, 30 percent; and persons of Hawaiian ancestry, 15 percent. Other groups represented are Filipinos, Chinese, Koreans, Samoans, and blacks, as well as other races and ethnic groups.

There are sixty-four entirely different racial combinations present in the state today. A fascinating photograph published in *National Geographic* magazine in 1924 showed thirty-two girls of the Kawaiahao Seminary, Honolulu, each of a different race or racial combination. These included Hawaiian; Ehu Hawaiian; Japanese; Chinese; Korean; Russian; Filipino; Portuguese; Polish-Russian; Hawaiian-German; Hawaiian-Chinese; Hawaiian-Russian; Hawaiian-American; Hawaiian-French; Hawaiian-Portuguese; Hawaiian-Filipino-Chinese; Hawaiian-Indian-American; Hawaiian-Japanese-Portuguese; Hawaiian-Portuguese-American; Hawaiian-Spanish-American; Hawaiian-German-Irish; Hawaiian-Spanish-German; Hawaiian-Chinese-American; Hawaiian-Portuguese-Irish; Hawaiian-Japanese-Indian; Hawaiian-Portuguese-Chinese-English; Hawaiian-Chinese-German-Norwegian-Irish; Nauru-Norwegian; African-French-Irish; Spanish-Puerto Rican; Guam-Mexican-French; and Samoan-Tahitian.

Descendants of Japanese, Filipinos, Chinese, and other laborers now hold leading places in corporations, government, the arts, and the professions.

The diversity of races in high positions is illustrated in the elected officials of the state. In the short period of statehood, there have been both Caucasian and Japanese governors, a Hawaiian-Caucasian lieutenant governor, Chinese and Japanese senators, and Caucasian, Hawaiian, and Japanese congressmen.

Hawaii has the reputation of being a model state, showing the harmonious blending of the races. There is almost no discrimination, and people live together with pleasure and respect. A good example of this is the Honolulu Symphony Orchestra. Its membership—all American citizens—has included Hawaiians, Koreans, blacks, Filipinos, Chinese, and Japanese, and Caucasians from America, Scandinavia, Portugal, Holland, Great Britain, and other lands.

More than 40 percent of the marriages in Hawaii each year are now inter-racial.

Religions in Hawaii are almost as diverse as races.

The first missionaries were Congregationalists. They were followed by Catholics, Mormons, Methodists, Anglicans, Lutherans, Seventh Day Adventists, Christian Scientists, Baptists, and others. The arrival of the first Chinese brought Confucianist, Taoist, and Buddhist worshippers. Japanese forms of worship, including five forms of Buddhism and also Shintoism, came with those from Japan. The first Jewish synagog was established in 1950. Today, the Roman Catholic church has the largest membership of any single religious group.

One-half of the entire population of Hawaii is under twenty-five years of age. Also, the average family in Hawaii, consisting of 4.29 persons, is the largest in the United States. Here indeed is a youthful, vigorous, culturally unique society. Yet even today, the influence of the original inhabitants who greeted all people as warmly as old friends, still pervades. Only the Hawaiians could have created their traditional slogan *O ke ola o ke kanaka,* which means "Humanity is above all nations."

Among the natural treasures of Hawaii are the nene (right), the rare Hawaiian goose that is the state bird. These fishermen (below) show off their catch of game fish from Hawaiian waters. Island blossoms (below right) are formed into beautiful leis for the pleasure of residents and visitors.

Natural Treasures

"A HUGE BOTANICAL GARDEN"

There are 650 species of plants and trees found nowhere else in the world except Hawaii. In addition, almost any type of flora will grow in Hawaii. As a result, Hawaii is like a huge botanical garden. The process of introducing most of the world's growing things into the islands began with the first Polynesians who brought useful and ornamental trees and plants on the long voyage in their canoes.

More than twenty-two thousand varieties of orchids alone grow in Hawaii. The state flower is the hibiscus, and there are more than five thousand varieties of hibiscus on the islands.

There are 130 species of ferns. One observer counted 35 species of ferns growing on the trunk of one fallen tree. Giant tree ferns tower up to forty feet (twelve meters) high, making beautiful fringes on the edges of many roads. There are 400,000 acres (161,874 hectares) of these tree ferns on the Big Island.

Some of the world's rarest plants grow in Hawaii. The incredible silversword plant with its six-foot (almost two-meter) silvery flower stalk grows only in the crater or on the slopes of Haleakala. The rare jade vine bears blue-green flower clusters, and the equally rare bombax has spectacular pink blossoms. The fragrant berries of mokihana grow only on Kauai. One of the universal favorites is the wood rose. Its dried pod resembles a carved rose blossom.

Edible plants and fruits are common. The most useful native starch plant is the taro, known as the Polynesian staff of life. Its tubers are cooked and pounded into poi, a pastelike pudding. Its food values are so high that doctors order it for invalids and infants.

The ti is one of the islands' most useful plants. Roasted, the ti root has the texture and taste of molasses candy; fermented, it is distilled into an alcoholic beverage. The leaves are used as wrappers for almost everything, as table cloths, and to make the "grass" hula skirts. A favorite sport is sliding down a grassy slope covered with ti leaves. Coconut trees provide ornament, shade, and a fruit containing a refreshing "milk" drink and tasty meat to be eaten alone or used in salads, candies, desserts, or toasted snacks. Husks make baskets for the growing of orchids, and scooped-out shells become highly polished food bowls.

Guavas are the most common wild fruit in the state. There are more than fifty kinds of bananas in Hawaii, of the eating variety and the cooking type, known as plantain. Papaya trees bear their edible melonlike fruit in a year's time after planting.

Of course, all Hawaiians say that nothing in the world tastes like fresh-picked Hawaiian pineapple.

Hawaii is aflame, especially in summer, with the brilliant colors of 460 varieties of ornamental trees. A photographer's delight is the shower tree. Entire Honolulu avenues are lined with these trees, which bear cascades of pink, yellow, or red bloom clusters. Highly prized is the rainbow shower tree, with its multicolored blooms. It has been named Honolulu's official tree. The blossom of the plumeria, or frangipani tree, is the most common of all flowers used in leis. The bright orange flower of the African tulip tree is admired most of the year. Feathery blooms of the lehua were sacred to the goddess Pele. These enchanting red pompons decorate the marvelous groves of native 'ohi'a trees in the rain forest. The waxlike flowers of the cup of gold are another delight—sometimes reaching a foot (thirty centimeters) in width.

Isabella Bird described "a burst of true tropical jungle palms, bread-fruit, candle-nuts of immense size, *koa*, bamboos, lianas climbing over the highest trees, stems as thick as a man's arm, candle-nuts with their pea-green and silver foliage, sandlewood, monkeypod, dark-leaved *koa,* the mahogany of the Pacific, the great glossy-leaved Eugenia, the small-leaved 'ohi'a. The forest soon became completely impenetrable . . . masses of matted vegetation carried us over streams six or eight feet below. I enjoyed it more than anything I have yet seen. It was a dream, a rapture, this maze of form and color, this entangled luxuriance."

Valuable and unusual nut trees also flourish. The *kukui* tree was invaluable to the early Hawaiians. Its nuts provide light oil, relishes, and medicine. Other parts of the tree can be used for dyes and the seeds for necklaces.

52

LIVING CREATURES

The state bird of Hawaii is the *nene* (pronounced nay-nay). This rare Hawaiian goose, the largest of the state's land birds, is an aquatic bird that has adapted itself to land. Today, there are only a small number of these unusual birds still living, but successful efforts are being made to preserve them.

The singing of many birds can be heard in Bird Park, a section of Hawaii Volcanoes National Park. Another bird sanctuary is at Kanaha, Maui. The Manhattan thrush is an imported bird of exquisite song. Many birds are visitors that migrate across the ocean for thousands of miles. These come from both Asia and the Americas to find their winter haven in Hawaii.

There are seven game birds in Hawaii, including gambel's quail, Rio Grande turkey, and chukkar partridge. A tremendously interesting variety of sea birds call Hawaii home. The islands at the far western end of the chain are especially rich in sea birds. Laysan Island is now a bird sanctuary and the nesting place for thousands of albatrosses.

Most of the island's animals have been imported, such as the pronghorn antelopes brought in from Montana. There are axis deer—natives of India and Ceylon—wild goats, wild boar, and mouflon, a wild sheep with large curling horns, a reddish brown coat, and greyish buff patches along the sides, introduced on the island of Lanai. Hunting seasons are open for deer, pig, wild goat, pheasant, and other game birds.

The waters off Hawaii abound with innumerable varieties of brilliant tropical fish, including a tiny fish with one of the longest names—the *humuhumunukunukuapua'a*. Some of the world's finest game fish are found in Hawaiian waters, including prize marlin, *mahimahi* (dolphin), swordfish and *aku* (skipjack). The sport of torch fishing, with flickering flames lighting the black waters, is a novel and exciting thrill for many enthusiasts.

Coral of great beauty and brilliance continues to grow in almost all Hawaiian waters. The Hawaiian black coral is one of the rarest of all the world's corals.

53

People Use Their Treasures

"FRUIT OF KINGS"

The most distinctive crop in Hawaii is the pineapple. The pineapple's existence was first recorded in Hawaii in 1813, growing wild. No one knows when it first came from Brazil, where pineapple is supposed to have originated.

In 1886 Captain John Kidwell, an English horticulturist, imported a thousand Smooth Cayenne, a superior variety of pineapples. Pineapples grew so well in Hawaii that soon there were far more than could be sold on the local market. In 1901, James Dole, a Harvard graduate who had come to Hawaii to make his fortune, set up the Hawaiian Pineapple Company (now Dole Corporation). He found a practical way to can pineapple so it could be shipped to faraway markets. In 1903 he packed about eighteen hundred cases.

Since that time the Dole company has become the largest fruit packing firm in the world; it owns the whole island of Lanai, which is devoted almost entirely to growing pineapple. Hawaii has become the world's greatest producer of pineapple. Eighty percent of all the pineapple consumed in the United States is grown there.

Pineapple growers cooperate in an association and in the Pineapple Research Institute, which helps to overcome diseases such as the wilt of 1930 that almost ended pineapple farming in Hawaii. The institute also works for new and improved growing and processing methods. As a result, the growing and canning of pineapple have become modern and efficient operations.

Pineapple is a tropical fruit that does not require a large amount of rainfall. The fruit grows on a plant with long, sharp leaves spiraling up around a short central stalk. Each new plant is started by planting a slip taken from near the base of the fruit or from a "sucker" taken from the stalk.

After the ground is prepared for planting, a machine lays black mulch paper in long rows and at the same time fumigates the soil

Opposite: A modern pineapple harvest.

beneath. The mulch paper conserves moisture, increases soil temperature, and discourages weeds.

A man—called a planter—pokes holes at regular intervals in the black paper and puts in slips—from 15,000 to 18,000 per acre (6,000 to 7,300 per hectare). The growing season is from eighteen to twenty-two months. After about fifteen months, a small bud about two or three inches (five to eight centimeters) long appears in the center of the plant. The bud has dozens of little blue and pink flowers. Nearly two years after the plant is set out, the first fruit ripens. Few sights are more beautiful than the straight rows of green and gold pineapple shining in Hawaii's deep red soil.

Picking is done by hand, and expert pickers can determine whether the fruit is ripe by the sound it makes when it is thumped. The picked fruit is carefully placed in long conveyor arms of a harvesting machine accompanying the pickers and then is rushed to the cannery. Almost every morsel of the pineapple is used. A machine called the Ginaca cuts off the ends and removes the shell and core all in one operation; the pineapple emerges as a golden cylinder ready for slicing or dicing.

Meanwhile, slips or suckers are taken from the plant for new plantings, and the old plant is left to bear a second crop of fruit, called the ratoon crop. After the second and sometimes third crop, the fields are plowed for another planting.

SUGAR IS SWEET AND GOOD FOR HAWAII

Sugarcane is a type of giant perennial grass. The early Hawaiians used it for a hedge, and Captain Cook reported finding sugar of "good quality" on his visit to Hawaii. Hawaii's sugar industry began with the first plantation and first mill on Kauai in 1835. Today, more than 236,000 acres (95,505 hectares) of Hawaii are devoted to sugar. The four largest islands produce a fifth of all sugar grown on United States soil. The yearly value of the Hawaiian sugar crop is almost $250 million, making sugar the most valuable crop in the state.

Hawaii is said to have the "most advanced sugar technology in the

Sugarcane fields on Maui.

world," and the growers work together closely in the Hawaiian Sugar Planters Association. Hawaiian sugarcane produces an average of ten tons (nine metric tons) of sugar an acre (four tons [more than three metric tons] per hectare)—the world's highest yield. No other area has made such full use of science, engineering, and mechanization in sugarcane production. Hawaiian planters pooled their money and skills to build irrigation systems that bring water from the rainy windward mountain heights to desert wastelands. Tunnels, ditches, wells, and canals have cost the planters more than $100 million. These planters have been called the "most daring and successful land reclaimers in the world." More than in any other sugar producing area, Hawaii has replaced grueling handwork with highly technical machines.

Planting to full ripeness requires from twenty-two to twenty-four months. Areas of higher elevation require a longer time period to bring sugarcane to its full sweetness. Because of the even climate, sugar is harvested in Hawaii during eight to ten months of the year

57

and trundled in huge cane haulers to the mills. There it moves through flashing knives that chop the cane into short pieces, which then pass through a series of high-pressure rollers to extract the juice. About 87 percent of the plant is sugar-bearing juice and only about 13 percent is plant fiber. The fiber, called bagasse, is used for fuel and to make wallboard and paper.

To prevent the loss of juice, the cane must be processed immediately; therefore, the mills never cease operation during the harvesting season. The process includes clarifying, filtering, evaporating, crystalizing, and centrifuging. In this way, Hawaii's mills turn out what is known as raw sugar, which is compact and nonperishable. Most of it is shipped to the mainland for refining. A by-product of sugar mills is blackstrap molasses, used in livestock feed. About 1 ton of molasses results from the manufacture of 4 tons of Hawaiian raw sugar (.9 metric ton of molasses from 3.6 metric tons of raw sugar).

OTHER AGRICULTURE

Hawaii is the only coffee-producing state of the union. The Kona region, in the shade of Mauna Loa, is considered an excellent region for raising mountain-grown coffee of exceptional quality.

Another crop new to the islands is the macadamia. This edible nut, with a unique flavor and texture, has been called by some the "most savory nut in the world." There is a rapidly expanding acreage and market for these nuts, amounting in Hawaii now to more than $5 million a year.

Vegetables and melons ($12 million), other fruits ($8 million), and taro ($1 million) are additional products of the islands.

About half a million packages of fresh flowers are shipped from Hawaii each year. Hawaii Island is the largest orchid-culture center in the United States, and Hilo is known as the Commercial Orchid Capital of the country.

Livestock, poultry, eggs, and dairy products account for state income of more than $35 million. The Parker ranch on Hawaii Island is the second largest in the United States. The picturesque cowboys of Hawaii are known as *paniolos*.

EARNING A LIVING

Manufacturing, in addition to that associated with sugar and pineapple, amounts to $500 million a year. An oil refinery, cement plant, steel mill, and pipe manufacturing plants are among the hundreds of manufacturing businesses in Hawaii.

One of the state's most colorful industries is the rapidly growing garment business. When the missionaries first came to the islands, they were shocked that the natives wore so few clothes. Once when an island couple was scolded for making a call without clothes, they went away and soon returned in shoes and stockings, with the man wearing a tall silk hat. In order to clothe the women, the missionaries concocted a Mother Hubbard-like garment that the people called mu'umu'u and the native women brightened with many colors.

Today, brightly colored dresses somewhat like the muumuu are in style all over the world. For many years the aloha shirt has been popular with men. The numerous peoples and cultures have influenced many Hawaiian garment designs, and the state's garment business now grosses several million dollars a year.

The manufacture of poi from the *taro* root is another interesting localized industry. Visitors at first are not greatly attracted to poi, a

Taro is one of the many crops that flourish in the Hawaiian Islands.

gray, unsalted paste. However, many people find it delicious, and it is very nourishing.

Small but interesting industries are based on the craft skills of the islanders. Many fine products are still woven from the dried leaves of *hala* (pandanus) trees. *Tikis,* feather *leis,* hand-printed silk fabrics, hula skirts, jewelry, handsome quilts, ceramics, woodenware, and many other skillfully made products are on display in local gift shops.

Fish are raised in many specially constructed ponds. Kewalo basin in Honolulu is home base for Hawaii's fishing fleet, and there are deep-water ports on all the major islands except Molokai. Gone, however, are the picturesque whaling fleets that centered in Hawaii after 1819. It is said that as many as 596 whaling ships might be at anchor at one time in the waters off Lahaina, Maui, and in the port of Honolulu.

Hawaii serves as the transportation hub of the Pacific. Honolulu International Airport is one of the busiest in the nation. The islands are interconnected by fine air service; service by barge also is utilized. The roads are good, but Hawaii's almost 4,000 miles (6,437 kilometers) of roads are the least extensive in the nation. The state's railroad system is also the nation's smallest.

In the field of communications, Hawaii had the first printing press in the nation west of the Rocky Mountains, set up by the missionaries. One of the first newspapers west of the Mississippi River was *Ka Lama Hawaii,* meaning "The Torch of Hawaii." The first English language newspaper began in 1836.

The first professional effort to interest tourists in Hawaii were undertaken in the 1920s. Today, Hawaii is one of the world's most popular vacationlands. The tourist industry brought in more than $1 billion to the state in 1976, as the number of tourists approached 3,500,000.

Another important factor in the economy of Hawaii is military spending. Altogether this brings about $500 million of personal income into the islands.

The per-family income of Hawaii is one of the highest in the nation. Costs of living are higher, but there are no heating fuel costs or seasonal clothing requirements.

Human Treasures

THOSE ROYAL HAWAIIANS

King Kamehameha the Great was born in the Kohala district on Hawaii Island, probably in 1758. Before he had reached the age of forty-five, he knew no more worlds to conquer. He ruled with a regal and sometimes despotic hand.

However, in comparison with earlier times, Kamehameha brought a "golden age" to Hawaii. He instituted laws against theft and murder and provided for courts that dispensed a primitive form of justice. He brought a temporary prosperity to the islands by depleting the supply of the wonderful aromatic sandalwood trees. This wood was greatly desired in China, and King Kamehameha cut and sold $400,000 worth of it to China in one year.

He remained devoted to the old religion. When some early visitors suggested that he turn to Christianity, the king asked them to demonstrate the power of their religion by throwing themselves off a cliff. Until they could do this without harm, he said, he intended to keep the old ways.

An interesting story is told of the eruption of Hualalai in 1801. Villages were destroyed, along with plantations and fish ponds. The terrified people called for the king, who arrived with a great retinue of priests and chiefs. They cut off some of the king's hair, which was considered sacred, and threw it into the advancing flow. In two days the lava flow ceased, and the king's reputation was greatly increased.

In accordance with ancient custom, when King Kamehameha died in 1819, his flesh was separated from his bones. The bones were carefully wrapped in tapa and concealed so well that his burial place has never been found. This secrecy was a part of the ancient tradition.

One of the most unusual persons in Hawaiian history is King Kaumualii of Kauai, who had paid tribute to Kamehameha the Great but remained independent. In 1821 Kamehameha II met Kaumualii at Waimea, Kauai, and invited him aboard the royal yacht. There the king of Kauai was made a prisoner and brought to Honolulu. He still

KAMEHAM

was recognized as king of his island, but was not permitted to return to his kingdom.

The enormous (300-pound or 136-kilogram) Queen Kaahumanu, widow of Kamehameha the Great, took a fancy to King Kaumualii, and they were married. For good measure, she also married Kaumualii's son, Prince Kealiiahonui. When the queen went out, she rode in her royal carriage, pulled by twelve of Kamehameha II's servants. Beside her rode her husband, the king of Kauai and, on the coachman's seat, her husband, the Prince of Kauai. The missionaries were probably most perplexed when this strangely mixed family attended church, as they often did.

The wife that King Kaumualii left behind, Queen Deborah Kapule, also weighed 300 pounds (136 kilograms). She stood 6 feet (183 centimeters) in height. When she became a convert to Christianity, Deborah Kapule demonstrated that she no longer feared the old gods by keeping her cows in a *heiau* (temple). After her husband was kidnapped, she became a leading personality on Kauai.

Many writers have told of the remarkable stature and physique of Hawaiian royalty and the *ali'i* (chiefs). Physically, and often mentally, they seemed to be a race apart.

MEN AND WOMEN WITH A MISSION

Missionary work among the lepers of Hawaii was begun in 1860 by the Reverend A.O. Forbes. Among the most famous missionaries on the islands was Father Damien, a Belgian. He went to the leper colony on Molokai in 1873 and devoted the rest of his life to caring for these afflicted people. Father Damien contracted the disease and died of its effects in 1889.

The Reverend Titus Coan, with headquarters at Hilo, confirmed twelve thousand carefully trained converts to Christianity during his many years there. He traveled constantly, climbing the *palis,* being let down by ropes from tree to tree and craig to craig. The Reverend

Opposite: This statue in Honolulu honors King Kamehameha the Great.

Coan crossed flooded rivers on the shoulders of a native, while men stretched themselves across the stream to keep him from being swept away. He became a renowned authority on volcanoes, with the irreverent nickname The High Priest of Pele.

Another Hawaii Island missionary was the Reverend Lorenzo Lyons. He devoted fifty-four years to traveling the island and bringing his message of religion. He wrote many hymns in the Hawaiian language and translated others, becoming known as the Poet of the Mountain Country.

Many missionaries became influential as cabinet officers in the government. William Richards served as an advisor to King Kamehameha III. Other missionary cabinet officers were Richard Armstrong and Dr. Gerrit P. Judd.

Those who have descended from the missionaries keep their memory alive at the Hawaiian Mission Children's Society.

SUCH INTERESTING PEOPLE

One of the favorite stories of Hawaii concerns the life of Koolau, the leper, as told in *The House of Pride* by Jack London. When lepers were being deported to Molokai, Koolau took refuge in the almost impenetrable valley of Kalalau on Kauai. Hiding with his family in the lava ridges, Koolau killed a deputy who had been sent to capture him. He held off a group of militia ordered to arrest him for murder. The militiamen left the valley thinking he was dead, and Koolau lived for five more years, cared for by his faithful wife who made many trips up the steep valley walls for supplies.

Another strange story of Kauai is that of Dr. George Scheffer, representative of the Russian Fur Company. He became the personal physician and great favorite of King Kaumualii of the island. He established himself in a thirty-acre (twelve-hectare) fortress on Kauai, and for a time much of the island was considered under Russian control, with the Russian flag flying over the King's palace. However, King Kaumualii finally grew tired of this situation and drove Dr. Scheffer and his Russian supporters from the island.

Elizabeth Sinclair emigrated from Scotland to New Zealand. After her husband died there, she managed their properties with great success, sold her lands, and set out on a clipper ship owned by her son-in-law to find a new home. In Hawaii she bought the entire island of Niihau from Kamehameha IV, along with a plantation on Kauai. Her greatest hope was to keep her large family together, which she managed to do. Today Niihau is still in the hands of her descendants, the Robinson family. The family has tried to maintain Niihau as it was in the 1800s, and they have been charmingly successful. There are no visitors except by invitation, no airplanes land there, and travel to the island is by sampan. This, of course, gives Niihau the reputation of an isle of mystery, and it is sometimes known as the Forbidden Island.

Among business people one of the most prominent was Charles Reed Bishop, founder of Bishop National Bank, now the First National Bank. He served King Lunalilo as foreign minister. James D. Dole's experiments led to the first successful canned pineapple pack. Harry Ginaca was another of those responsible for Hawaii's pineapple success. In 1912 as an engineer with Dole, he invented the Ginaca machine for shelling and coring the fruit. Benjamin F. Dillingham developed sugar plantations and a railroad on Oahu. His son, Walter F. Dillingham, supervised wide-scale dredging operations, including the establishment of Pearl Harbor.

The dean of Hawaii's artists is noted painter Madge Tennent. A native of South Africa, Madge Tennent came to the islands after studying in Paris. One critic asserted that "Even if the Hawaiians were to vanish as a race they would live forever in the paintings of Madge Tennent." She is known as the Gauguin of Hawaii.

Other important artists include Isami Doi, Willson Y. Stamper, Tseng Yu-ho, Huc Mazelet Luquiens, John Kelly, A.S. (Sam) MacLeod, D. Howard Hitchcock, Ben Norris, Joseph Feher, and Fritz Abplanalp.

Hawaii has had some famous swimmers. Duke Kahanamoku won the 100-meter freestyle event in the 1912 and 1920 Olympic Games and Keo Nakama was the first person to make the grueling swim from Molokai to Oahu.

The Kamehameha Schools on Kapalama Heights in Honolulu.

Teaching and Learning

In the field of education, Hawaii has many distinctions. Lahainaluna High School, established by the missionaries on Maui in 1831, is the oldest high school west of the Rocky Mountains. By 1832 there were 900 schools, each with its missionary teacher, enrolling 54,000 pupils, mostly adults. In 1841 the missionaries established Punahou School for missionary children, and a royal school was set up to train children of the royal families.

Among the nation's leading private schools are the Kamehameha schools on Kapalama Heights in Honolulu, supported solely from revenues of the vast Bishop estate, of which the institutions are the sole beneficiary. These schools, begun in 1887, limit their enrollment to children of Hawaiian ancestry. A superbly qualified staff of 150 works with 2,000 students on a beautiful landscaped campus of 80 acres (32 hectares) in a modern educational environment. Their great Hawaiian heritage is stressed to the students. Another outstanding preparatory school is Mid-Pacific Institute of Honolulu.

The public school system of Hawaii is the only one in the nation run as a state-wide operation, rather than by individual boards of education. The median education level of Hawaii is above the national average.

The University of Hawaii is one of the newest of the main state universities. It was founded in 1907 as an agricultural college. The university has one of the most varied student bodies in the world. Its location makes it ideal for a number of specialized programs. The East-West Center at the university promotes cultural and technical interchanges between East and West.

One of the outstanding centers of its kind is the university's Geophysics Institute. The university operates a marine laboratory on Moku O Loe Island off Oahu. The University of Hawaii Press is an important publishing company.

The University of Hawaii operates a branch at Hilo, and there are four private colleges in Hawaii: Hawaii Pacific College, the Hawaii campus of Brigham Young University, Hawaii Loa College, and Chaminade College, all on Oahu.

Enchantment of Hawaii

HO'OKIPA MAI: COME AND BE FRIENDLY

"I am now convinced that I have never seen anything so perfectly lovely . . . I could remain forever on such enchanted shores." An early traveler wrote this about Hawaii, and visitors have been echoing the sentiment ever since. Hawaii is the dream vacationland not only of mainland Americans but people from many parts of the world. For example, Hawaii was the choice of most Japanese who listed their "dream vacation" for a survey.

The islands have activities, sights, and customs completely different from the continental lands. Hawaii provides a fascinating combination of the old Polynesian culture with the new tropical American civilization. Here people do not dash through life. In this land the spirit of aloha lingers. Aloha is a greeting, a farewell, thanks, love, goodwill. Isabella Bird wrote, "Aloha represents to me all of kindness and goodwill that language can express, and the convenience of it as compared with other phrases is that it means exactly what the receiver understands it to mean."

In Hawaii the visitor can engage in outrigger canoe riding, deep-sea fishing, spearfishing, skin diving, and scuba diving in ideal settings. Vacationers can combine incomparable scenery with the unusual offerings of the islands.

This is a land where the people are courteous, and the way of life is gracious.

MOST EXCITING, MOST EXOTIC

Just a few hours by jet from California is one of America's most exciting and exotic cities. Arriving at Honolulu, most visitors are likely to think that all the races and half the flowers of Hawaii are

To many tourists, Hawaii means Waikiki Beach (opposite).

Hawaii's capitol building in Honolulu, supported by twenty-four graceful columns, rests in a reflecting pool.

concentrated there. Actually, the city and county of Honolulu contain 80 percent of the state's entire population. Legend indicates that Honolulu was founded about 1100 A.D., which in one sense makes it America's oldest city.

Honolulu's civic center is particularly interesting. Here is historic Iolani ("Heavenly Bird") Palace, once the capitol building of Hawaii. It was built by King Kalakaua and finished in 1882 at a cost of $350,000. The Hawaiian legislature met there. The building is the only royal palace and contains the only throne room under United States jurisdiction. Its interior is noted for fine exotic woods. Queen Liliuokalani was held under house arrest in Iolani Palace after being deposed. Earlier, while a princess, she composed one of the world's most famous songs—"Aloha Oe."

Quaint Iolani Barracks, where the royal "troops" were housed, was removed to a new location on the palace grounds, where it is now a prime tourist attraction. The Governor's House, "Washington Place," is known as the Little White House of the Pacific.

Hawaii now possesses the nation's most unusual capitol building. The entire structure rests in a pool on twenty-four graceful columns. Entrance is by a bridge. The ornamental grille work and many openings give the building the appearance of almost complete openness.

70

The Kahili Room of the Bishop Museum is a fascinating place. Here are displayed part of the museum's fabulous collection of twenty-six feather robes. One of these is referred to as the "million dollar" feather cloak. The museum has priceless collections of materials made and used in Hawaii before historic times. The Kilolani Planetarium is on the museum grounds.

The Honolulu Academy of Arts ranks with the world's foremost art museums of its size. It is said to be the only complete art museum in the entire Pacific region. Its displays of Oriental and Pacific art are especially notable.

Other museums are the Queen Emma Museum, in the former summer palace of Queen Emma, the University of Hawaii Art Gallery, and the Tennent Art Foundation. The Fine Art Gallery in the Hawaiian Village also occasionally features prominent collections.

Another cultural treasure of the islands is the Honolulu Symphony, founded in 1898. It gives frequent concerts in the concert hall of the Neil Blaisdell Center and in tours of the neighboring islands. The Honolulu Community Theater often gets first non-professional rights to some of the best plays and musical comedies from the mainland. Producers grant these rights to Hawaii long before giving them to nonprofessional groups on the mainland. The University of Hawaii is also noted for its theater group.

Foster Botanic Garden provides a collection of rare tropical plants. Its fascinating orchid greenhouse sparked the orchid industry of the islands. The park was the former home of Hawaii's first botanist, William Hillebrand. Wonderful Kapiolani Park contains the Honolulu Zoo, housing one of the world's largest tropical bird collections. Another of the world's greatest collections—an exhibit of marine life—is found at Sea Life Park.

Honolulu is one of the greatest of all shopping centers. Some visitors are amazed by Hawaii's modern stores. The Shirokiya Department Store in the Ala Moana Center was built in Japan, knocked down and reassembled on Oahu. The largest collection of Japanese ware east of Tokyo is said to be found in S.M. Iidas' Japanese stores.

The International Market Place displays craft and art work of the Pacific in typical settings, such as grass-thatched houses and bamboo stalls. In the village of Ulu Mau the Hawaiian people show their way of life and display their arts and crafts. On a wider scale, the same is done for Hawaiian, Maori, Tongan, Fijian, Tahitian, and Samoan cultures in the Polynesian Cultural Center at Laie on Oahu.

Contrasting with the commercial buildings are the churches. Kawaiahao Church is known as the Westminster Abbey of Hawaii, because royal coronations were held there. For construction of the church, each Christian native brought a block of rock coral, a total of fourteen thousand stones. It was the first church in the islands and was the chapel of kings. Services are still given in both English and Hawaiian.

The First Methodist Church of Honolulu, an architectural contrast, is one of the best examples of modern architecture in Hawaii. The First Chinese Christian Church provides a charming reminder of the Orient with its pagoda steeple and Chinese style. Syngman Rhee, Korean president during the Korean War, founded the Korean Christian Church in Honolulu when he was in exile there. It is interesting to note that when Rhee was again forced into exile from South Korea, he chose Hawaii once more and died there in 1965. The Makiki Japanese Christian Church resembles a Japanese castle.

The royal mausoleum contains the bodies of all members of the Kamehameha line except Kamehameha the Great, whose burial place is unknown.

Other Honolulu structures of interest are the Aloha Tower, Neil Blaisdell Center with its municipal auditorium seating 11,000, and the Ilikai, a combined apartment house and hotel, with its outdoor glass-enclosed elevator. This gives a view of the city and harbor on the way to the rooftop restaurant.

Few cities are changing or growing faster than Honolulu, but even so the city keeps its distinctive touch.

To many tourists, Hawaii means Waikiki Beach, and here are found all the conveniences of the best hotels with some of the world's finest water sports.

One of the most enchanting times to see Honolulu is during one of the many festivals. Aloha Week, the annual festival recalling the

Aerial view of Waikiki Beach and Diamond Head.

pageantry of the kings and queens, is one of the most popular. There are the Narcissus, Cherry Blossom, and other Polynesian and Filipino festivals. Great quantities of evergreens are imported for Christmas, and on New Year's Eve the celebrants explode fireworks under certain safety restrictions.

Several hundred of the finest hula dancers, from age two to seventy, gather in August for the annual Hula Festival at Waikiki Shell in Kapiolani Park. The hula is one of the world's most graceful dances, and it tells a story in pantomime. The stories range from the most dignified to the ridiculous. The hula was originally a religious expression and was taught at a special school called a *halau*. There the students learned about two hundred different hulas and many of the old songs called *meles*.

Another must for visitors is the luau, the native Hawaiian feast, or for a few lucky visitors the *'aha'aina,* a native feast on an even grander scale. The main course of a luau is the pig roasted whole in an underground pit. Red hot rocks, placed around and in the pig and the rest of the food, provide the heat. Some people are able to place the red hot rocks in the pig with their bare hands. The roasted meats

This view from Nuuanu Pali, Oahu, is spectacular.

and vegetables, wrapped in ti-leaf packets, are served with coconut pudding, fresh pineapple, shellfish, and other exotic dishes on ti-leaf covered tables, dotted with bright island flowers. Poi, of course, is served as the chief starch food. There is authentic Hawaiian music and hula dancing at a luau.

THE REST OF OAHU

The word Oahu means The Gathering Place. Today the island's population density of 1,254 persons per square mile (484 per square kilometer) is greater than that of Japan or the British Isles, and yet some of Oahu is still more or less as the first European saw it. Visitors to Oahu are especially pleased that the women of the Outdoor Circle have been able to keep advertising billboards entirely off Oahu so that the superb scenery is unspoiled.

Hawaii's most popular scenic lookout is probably the famed Nuuanu Pali. The gorgeous panoramic vista of windward Oahu from this lofty, historic windswept cliff has been called one of the "scenic wonders of the world." Visitors may imagine the anguished cries of the Oahu warriors as they were forced to their deaths over the *pali* by Kamehameha I's conquering army. Another beautiful scenic area is the drive along the eastern seacoast of the island from Koko Head to Makapuu Point.

The National Memorial Cemetery of the Pacific in Puowaina (Punchbowl) Crater—Hill of Sacrifice—honors the dead of World War II. Here, more than seventeen thousand victims of recent wars are buried, including war correspondent Ernie Pyle.

Kukaniloko near Wahiawa is the site of sacred birthstones where certain Hawaiian chiefesses gave birth to the royal princes and princesses.

Makapuu Beach is considered one of the world's best for body surfing. At Laie visitors may participate in hukilau fishing. An enormous net is placed in the sea, and as many people as possible draw in the entrapped fish, while others prepare for the luau. One of the world's most picturesque Mormon temples is also located at Laie.

75

World-renowned military posts and installations on Oahu include Pearl Harbor, probably the finest naval base anywhere, and Schofield Barracks, established in 1909 and now one of the largest permanent army posts in the United States.

HAWAII: THE ORCHID ISLAND

Hawaii is the largest island in the Hawaiian chain, the one from which the whole group takes its name. Much of what remains of the old Polynesian culture of the islands is found on Hawaii. The Kona district of Hawaii is said to be "everyone's dream of a South Pacific Island—temple ruins in the moonlight, early morning swims in quiet coves, isolated villages and miles of some of the thickest, brightest foliage in all the islands." Hulihee Palace, in Kona, where Hawaiian kings had their summer home, is now a museum.

Hilo is the City of Orchids. Hundreds of thousands of blooms are mailed out each year. However, the name Hilo itself means "new moon," and comes from the crescent shape of its bay. The Lyman House at Hilo, a large frame house of a missionary family, has been made into a museum.

The old sacred City of Refuge in Honaunau has been restored as a National Historical Park. The foundation of the temple found here is thought to have been built in the twelfth century. All who entered were given refuge in time of war or forgiven for breaking the laws. The Painted Church at Honaunau is the first Catholic church in Hawaii.

At Kapaau is Kalahikiola Church. Father Bond, the pastor, described its construction: "The stones were gathered from neighboring ravines and brought on men's shoulders. Men in canoes with ropes and sticks for loosening up the bunches of coral would go into three or four fathoms of water. Wood for burning it was brought for eight or ten miles ... hundreds of barrels of sand were brought by women and children from all along the coast in bits of *kapa,* small

76

Guardian Ki'i (Images) at City of Refuge National Historical Park.

calabashes, or small *lauhala* bags.'' Six years of such strenuous labor were needed to finish the church.

A monument has been erected in memory of Captain Cook near where he fell at Kealakekua Bay. Another seaside attraction of the Big Island is the black-sand beach near Kalapana, where white surf foams in ever changing patterns on the jet black shores.

The two great volcanoes that created Hawaii dominate the island. The sight of Mauna Loa and Mauna Kea, mantled with snow during the winter, looming against the dark blue tropical sky, is unforgettable. Here, surprisingly, is fantastically good skiing.

Mauna Loa and Kilauea, the crater part way up its slope, make up the Hawaii Volcanoes National Park. The park headquarters is near Kilauea Crater, and there is volcano museum. A hotel, Volcano House, rests on the crater rim, giving an awesome view into the crater. A road circles the crater top, and trails lead past steaming cracks in the ground and into Bird Park, a wildlife sanctuary. Still growing are the sacred berries of the goddess Pele—the *ohelo*. They remain "sacred" since they can't be picked in a national park. Visitors can walk through the Thurston Lava Tube.

Another awesome natural spectacle is sometimes visible at Volcano House. When dawn comes over Mauna Loa on a clear day, the pink sunlight occasionally appears to be sweeping down the slope in what is called a "rose mantle."

Mauna Loa and Kilauea are among the world's most spectacular volcanoes in eruption and the most harmless to life. Countless people rush to see them when they are active—climbing as near as possible or flying over in special planes.

English travel writer Isabella Bird in 1873 was one of the first non-native women to reach the summit crater of Mauna Loa. Her party crossed the flat tableland of the top by horseback. She said about this trip over the hard, spiked lava: "The mules with their small legs and wonderful agility were more frightened than hurt, but the horses were splashed with blood up to their knees, and their poor eyes looked piteous." They arrived when the volcano was slightly active. "A fountain of pure yellow fire, unlike the red gleam of Kilauea, was regularly playing in several united but independent jets, throwing up its glorious incandescence to a height of 150 to 300 feet, at one time 600! You cannot imagine such a beautiful sight."

Today, the more rugged traveler can hike to the top, or special trucks can be used to ascend Mauna Loa, but arrangements must be made in advance.

Opposite: Spectacular Akaka Falls on the island of Hawaii plunges more than 400 feet (122 meters) to the pool below.

The same inner fires threw up Mauna Kea to the highest point in Hawaii, 13,796 feet (4,205 meters), but they have long been dormant. The summit of this great mountain is the site of an astronomical observatory.

A noted American met a strange death on Mauna Kea in 1834. The famed naturalist David Douglas, for whom the Douglas fir is named, was found dead in a bullock pit in a mystery that has never been solved.

Haleakala National Park, Maui.

"MAUI NO KA OI": MAUI IS THE BEST

Maui is named for the demigod Maui who by legend fished up the Hawaiian Islands from the sea. Another legend says that from the crater of Haleakala (now a national park) Maui captured the sun and held him captive until he promised to slow down his journey and give the Hawaiians more time to carry on their daily tasks.

Even beginning riders can make the horseback trip into the world's largest extinct crater. They may see two of the earth's rarest natural phenomena—the strange silversword plant, one species of which grows only in Haleakala crater, and the Specter of the Brocken. The Brocken is a peak in Germany and the only other place in the world where the specter appears. This specter becomes visible when cloud formations and the sun are exactly right. Then the visitor's shadow appears on the nearby clouds, surrounded by a circular rainbow.

Science City on Haleakala houses a satellite tracking station, solar observatory, an "air-glow" observatory, and ballistics missile observatory.

The coastline of Maui is one of the most spectacular anywhere. Maui's west coast has been compared to the famous Amalfi drive in Italy. The Keanae Road is another spectacular ocean drive.

One of the most historic places in the state is Lahaina, capital of the old kings and once the whaling capital of the world. It is being carefully restored to retain its historic appearance. Lahainaluna High School, the first high school west of the Rockies, still operates here. Missionaries operated the first printing press and published one of the first newspapers west of the Mississippi at Lahaina.

In Wainee Cemetery are buried Queen Keopuolani, ranking wife of Kamehameha I and mother of the second and third Kamehamehas, and another wife of Kamehameha I, Queen Kalakua, from whom Kamehameha IV, V, and Lunalilo were all descended. In the royal cemetery also are the remains of King Kaumualii of Kauai.

Another historic site is Iao Valley, where Kamehameha I fought the victorious battle for the control of Maui. The landmark of the valley and one of the strangest formations anywhere is the volcanic spire called Iao Needle, towering 2,250 feet (686 meters) from the valley floor.

Hale Hoikeike, once a missionary seminary for girls at Wailuku, is now a museum. It contains old calabashes and furniture carved in the old days from fine woods. *Tapas* and stone instruments of ancient times are displayed there. The building itself was made with plaster strengthened by clippings of students' hair.

The Seven Sacred Pools, connected by a ribbonlike cascade, is the site where the mother of the god Maui is said to have washed her *tapa* clothing.

KAUAI (GARDEN ISLAND) AND NIIHAU

One of the country's most spectacular sights is Waimea Canyon, the Grand Canyon of Hawaii, on Kauai. The grandeur of its depths and the jewel tones of its colors make the canyon an outstanding natural spectacle. The high point of a visit is the view from Kalalau Lookout.

Waimea Valley has many typical Hawaiian attractions: *taro* patches, a poi factory, a cane field, rice paddies, churches of Buddhist and Mormon faiths, and even the supposed work of the Menehune. There are also the remains of a prehistoric Hawaiian village, with a quiet pool nearby. In this pool was said to dwell the nymph Kamalio, who appeared only to male humans, combing her jet-black hair by the pool's edge. Women could not see her at all.

The ruins of an historic old Russian fort built by Dr. George A. Scheffer lie near the mouth of Waimea River.

Kauai possesses rushing streams and other results of the greatest rainfall in the world. Many of the swift-running streams are stocked with trout, and the island is divided by a multitude of valleys—each one a garden of loveliness.

Opposite: The Iao Needle is a volcanic spire that towers above the Iao Valley floor, where Kamehameha I fought the battle for control of Maui.

The Wailua River is known as the Sacred Water because of the number of *heiaus* along its banks. Holo-Holo-Ku Heiau is among the oldest of the temples, built in honor of the war god Ku, who required a human sacrifice before every battle. The ancient sacrificial stone where bodies were tied may still be viewed. This temple has been restored by the Kauai Historical Society and the Bishop Museum.

Near the Wailua River stands the famed coconut grove and lagoon, home of royalty for six hundred years, which has been carefully preserved by the Coco Palms Hotel. Sleeping Giant, another Kauai landmark, is a ridge of hills that from a distance appears very much like a huge figure asleep on its back.

Another interesting stream and valley is Kealia. Nearby Waipahee Falls contains the famous slide where swimmers cascade down the smooth slope of a broken lava tube. St. Catherine's Roman Catholic Church is located in the valley. Its murals were painted by three of Hawaii's leading artists.

Waioli Mission, near Hanalei, was built in a combination of New England and Hawaiian styles that is influencing Hawaiian architecture even today. Isabella Bird said of the Hanalei region: "Indeed for mere loveliness that part of Kauai exceeds anything I have ever seen."

The burnished gold sands of Haena beach were turned into the island of Bali when the motion picture *South Pacific* was made. Its Bali Ha'i scenes were shot there in the shadow of the steep blue-green *palis* (cliffs). *South Pacific* scenes were also filmed at Kilauea and other scenic spots on Kauai.

Makahuena Point has an interesting history. Here, boards and other flotsam and jetsam that drifted to the islands from the Americas brought along nails and hooks, greatly prized by the Hawaiians.

Floating like an amethyst on the blue Pacific off the coast of Kauai is the privately owned island of Niihau. On it live about two hundred pure-blooded Hawaiians. They were noted for their fine handwoven mats and the island shores are renowned for their wonderful variety of shells. Visitors may go to Niihau only by the invitation of the owners, the Robinson family.

THE OTHER ISLANDS

The Hawaiian influence is also felt on Molokai, the least spoiled of the major islands—the Friendly Island—where people of 50 percent or more Hawaiian blood were given homesteads. Until recently the Hawaiians in the Halawa Valley lived much as their ancestors did. Here the fine fish nets were woven and thrown with great skill into the ocean; poi was pounded and the ancient crops were planted in the old ways. The sacred kukui grove planted by Kahuna Lanikaula is one of the most revered spots in all Hawaii.

Many parts of Molokai are devoted to ranching, and there is a strong similarity to ranch lands of the mainland. Kaunakakai is the principal town of the island.

The northern coast of Molokai is walled off by a 2,000-foot (610-meter) high *pali* that can be approached only by boat. Its scenery is magnificent.

On the Kalaupapa Peninsula is the Hansen's disease settlement. Lepers were isolated here in earlier times. Now patients can be treated and generally cured through the use of the most modern facilities. They receive a subsidy from the government for their necessities and a few luxuries such as movies. Most of the cured patients remain at Kalaupapa. New patients are no longer being admitted, and in time there will be no leper colony. Meanwhile, visitors are welcome.

Northern coastline, Molokai.

Shipwreck Beach, on the north shore of Lanai, is a beachcomber's paradise.

A monument to the leper priest, Father Damien, who gave his life for his afflicted adopted people, stands at Kalaupapa.

Lanai, the Pineapple Island, has fewer tourists than the other islands, although they are welcome. It is owned by the Dole Corporation. The company has built Lanai City as a model town of the plantation type. Dole also built roads, irrigation projects, and the million-dollar harbor of Kaumalapau, where the fruit of a million pineapples can be loaded into barges in a day.

The ancient village of Kaunolu, now a ghost town, was once the summer residence of Kamehameha the Great. Nearby is Kahekili's Jump. Here Kamehameha is supposed to have disciplined his soldiers by making them dive sixty feet (eighteen meters) into the sea. This was not so difficult for men who lived almost as much in the water as on land, but halfway down was a shelf of rock projecting out for fifteen feet (five meters), which required a great leap to avoid being dashed to pieces. Many of Kamehameha's soldiers failed to make it, so the story goes.

Shipwreck Beach on the north shore of Lanai is a beachcomber's paradise. Here in an eight-mile (thirteen-kilometer) stretch can be found driftwood and other articles possibly from the farthest reaches of the globe. The quaint dwellings of Driftwood Village have been devised almost entirely from driftwood.

Kahoolawe Island is uninhabited. During and after World War II it has been used as a target by the United States fleet and bombers. Its barren red slopes contain unexploded bombs, giving good reason for its nickname of the Island of Death or, more commonly, Target Island.

THE LANGUAGE OF HAWAII

To those accustomed to English and other modern languages, the Hawaiian speech sounds strange and totally unfamiliar. The vowel sounds seem to come tumbling out in a way that most *malihinis* (newcomers) cannot imitate easily. Trying to say two i's together or a long word in which there may be only one or two consonants seems almost impossible at first. However, the Hawaiians master it with a smooth, flowing ease.

There are only twelve letters in the Hawaiian alphabet, the five vowels with seven consonants added: h, k, l, m, n, p, and w. Some of these do double duty. In chanting, k becomes t. This musical language contains none of the raspings found in other languages.

Wai is the word for water; combined with other words it becomes Wailuku or Waialeale ("rippling water") or Waioli ("singing water"). *Mauna* is the word for mountain, and saying Mauna Loa is simply to say Mount Loa in Hawaiian, or "long mountain." Many words such as *aloha* and *pilikia* have varieties of meanings. Anyone in a *pilikia* could be in big trouble or only in a slight difficulty.

A notable feature of the language is that all syllables and all words end in vowels.

Pidgin English, a combination of English and Hawaiian with words and intonations from other languages, is the bane of the English teachers, but many Hawaii residents lapse into it on occasion. Even the very well educated are generally proud of their ability to communicate in pidgin.

No matter what language the people of Hawaii speak—English, Hawaiian, Portuguese, Chinese, Japanese, Korean, pidgin—there is one thing on which they all agree: they live in an enchanted world, the best of all possible lands.

Handy Reference Section

Instant Facts

Became 50th state August 21, 1959
Capital—Honolulu, 1804
Nickname—The Aloha State
State motto— *Ua Mau Ke Ea O Ka Aina I Ka Pono* ("The life of the land is
         perpetuated in righteousness")
State bird—Nene (Hawaiian goose)
State tree—Candlenut *(Kukui)*
State song—"Hawaii Ponoi" (unofficial), by King Kalakaua, music by Henry
         Berger
Area—6,450 square miles (16,705 square kilometers)
Rank in area—47th
Coastline—750 miles (1,207 kilometers)
Shoreline—1,052 miles (1,693 kilometers)
Extent of the archipelago (southeast to northwest)—1,523 miles (2,451
         kilometers)
Geographic center—20° 15' N, 156° 20' W (off Maui Island)
Highest point—13,796 feet (4,205 meters), Mauna Kea, island of Hawaii
Lowest point—Sea level
Number of counties—5
Population—965,000 (1980 census)
Rank in population—39th
Population density—150 per square mile (58 per square kilometer), 1980 census
Rank in density—17th
Population center—In Honolulu County, in Kauwi Channel, 15.2 miles (24.5
         kilometers) southeast of Honolulu
Birthrate—18.2 per 1,000 persons
Infant mortality rate—15.3 per 1,000 births
Physicians per 100,000—163

Principal cities—		
Honolulu	365,048	(1980 census)
Pearl City	42,575	
Kailua	35,812	
Hilo	35,269	
Kaneohe	29,919	
Waipahu	29,139	

You Have a Date with History

1778—Captain James Cook arrived in Hawaii
1792—First visit by Captain George Vancouver
1795—Kamehameha I conquered all islands except Kauai and Niihau

You Have a Date with History

1797—Law of the Splintered Paddle protected persons on highways
1819—Kamehameha I died; *kapu* abolished by Kamehameha II
1820—First American missionaries arrived
1840—First written constitution
1843—Hawaiian independence recognized
1848—Great *Mahele*, division of lands
1859—First gas lighting
1878—First telephones
1883—Iolani Palace completed
1893—Monarchy overthrown
1894—Republic of Hawaii established
1898—Annexation by United States
1900—Territorial government established
1903—First successful pineapple pack
1927—First flight from mainland
1936—Regular passenger air service
1941—Pearl Harbor attacked
1950—Mauna Loa activity produces largest lava flow in modern times
1959—Statehood
1965—Omnibus Education Bill
1968—New state constitution is adopted
1969—New state capitol is completed
1974—First governor of Japanese descent of any state installed
1976—Tourists number more than three million

Individual Islands

Name	Width east-west		Length north-south		Area		Highest Point		Population 1980 census
	mi.	km.	mi.	km.	sq. mi.	sq. km.	feet	meters	
Hawaii	93	150	76	122	4,038	10,458	13,796	4,205	92,053
Maui	48	77	26	42	729	1,888	10,023	3,055	62,823
Oahu	44	71	30	48	608	1,575	4,040	1,231	762,874
Kauai	33	53	25	40	553	1,432	5,170	1,576	38,856
Molokai	38	61	10	16	261	676	4,970	1,515	6,049
Lanai	18	29	13	21	140	363	3,370	1,027	2,119
Niihau	18	29	6	10	73	189			226
Kahoolawe	11	18	6	10	45	117	1,477	450	none
Minor islets					3	8			none

Rulers of Hawaii

King Kamehameha I (Paiea)	1795-1819
King Kamehameha II (Liholiho)	1819-1824
King Kamehameha III (Kauikeaouli)	1824-1854
King Kamehameha IV (Alexander Liholiho)	1854-1863
King Kamehameha V (Lot)	1863-1872
King Lunalilo (William Charles)	1873-1874
King Kalakaua (David)	1874-1891
Queen Lilioukalani (Lydia)	1891-1893

President of the Republic

Sanford Ballard Dole	1894-1898

Governors of the Territory   1900-1959

Governors of the State of Hawaii

William Francis Quinn	1959-1962
John Anthony Burns	1962-1974
George R. Ariyoshi	1974-

Chinaman's Hat, Kaawa, Oahu.

Selected Hawaiian Words

Pronunciation: A is pronounced as in *alone;* E as in *sleigh;* I as in *chlorine;* O as in *go;* U as in *blue.* In general, Hawaiian words are pronounced in much the same way as Latin or Romance languages. Consonants are usually as in English. W is pronounced as V at the start of some words; however, this is not true in either the words Hawaii or Waikiki. Usually Hawaiian words are accented on the next to the last syllable. When the second syllable of a word is a double vowel or diphthong, the second syllable receives the accent. The hamzah (') or glottal stop indicates that the letter "k" has been omitted.

'Ae: yes
'Aha'aina: feast
'Aina: land
Ali'i: chief
Aloha: greeting, farewell
'A'ole: no
Hale: dwelling
Hana: act of working
Heiau: temple
Hiamoe: act of sleeping
Holoku: princess-style dress with train
Holomu'u: holoku with no train
Ho'omanawanui: relax, take it easy
Hui: club or association
'Ilio: dog
Ka: the (article)
Kalo: taro
Kana: man or humanity
Kane: man or husband
Kapa: bark cloth
Kapu: sacred, forbidden
Kilu: game
Kona: south
Kupa: native
Lae: cape of land
Lanai: terrace or porch
Lani: heaven
Lei: flower wreath

Lu'au: kalo leaves, a feast
Mahalo: thanks
Makai: seaward
Malihini: newcomer
Manawa 'ole: in no time
Manawahi: no charge, free
Mauka: inland
Mauna: mountain
Mele: song
Menehune: legendary dwarfs
Mo'o: lizard or snake
Moana: ocean
Mu'umu'u: loosely fitted dress
Pali: cliff
Pau: completed, finished
Pa'u: riding skirt
Pilikia: difficulty, disaster
Poi: paste puddings
Poi'o: head
Pua'a: hog
Puka: hole
Pupule: insane, crazy
Ua: rain
Wa'a: canoe
Wahine: female, woman
Wai: fresh water
Wauke: paper mulberry
Wikiwiki: hurry

Index

92

94

PICTURE CREDITS

Color photographs courtesy of the following: American Airlines, pages 2-3, 21, 31; Panorama Air Tour, Inc., 8; Hawaii Visitors Bureau, 13, 18, 19, 23, 25, 27, 28 (bottom), 36, 41, 42, 47, 50 (left and bottom right), 57, 62, 66, 70, 73, 74, 79, 80, 83, 85, 86, 90; American Museum of Natural History, 14; United Air Lines, 15, 68; City of Refuge National Historical Park, 22, 77; Smithsonian Institution, 28 (top); USDI, Fish and Wildlife Service, Luther C. Goldman, 50 (top right); US Department of Agriculture, 54; USDA, Robert Hailstock, 59.

Illustrations on back cover by Len W. Meents.

ABOUT THE AUTHOR

With the publication of his first book for school use when he was twenty, **Allan Carpenter** began a career as an author that has spanned more than 135 books. After teaching in the public schools of Des Moines, Mr. Carpenter began his career as an educational publisher at the age of twenty-one when he founded the magazine *Teachers Digest*. In the field of educational periodicals, he was responsible for many innovations. During his many years in publishing, he has perfected a highly organized approach to handling large volumes of factual material: after extensive traveling and having collected all possible materials, he systematically reviews and organizes everything. From his apartment high in Chicago's John Hancock Building, Allan recalls, "My collection and assimilation of materials on the states and countries began before the publication of my first book." Allan is the founder of Carpenter Publishing House and of Infordata International, Inc., publishers of *Issues in Education* and *Index to U. S. Government Periodicals*. When he is not writing or traveling, his principal avocation is music. He has been the principal bassist of many symphonies, and he managed the country's leading non-professional symphony for twenty-five years.